To Da[...]

Christmas 2000

from

Jerry and Donna

Helsey

I ALMOST MISSED THE SUNSET

My Perspectives on Life and Music

BILL GAITHER
with JERRY JENKINS

Publishers Since 1798

THOMAS NELSON PUBLISHERS
Nashville

Published in Nashville, Tennessee, by Thomas Nelson, Inc.,

Scripture quotations are from the NEW KING JAMES VERSION of the Bible. Copyright © 1979, 1980, 1982, Thomas Nelson, Inc., Publishers.

Library of Congress Cataloging-in-Publication Data

Gaither, Bill.
    I almost missed the sunset : my perspectives on life and music / William J. Gaither with Jerry B. Jenkins.
        p.   cm.
    ISBN 0-8407-7573-3
    1. Gaither, Bill. 2. Gospel musicians—United States—Biography. I. Jenkins, Jerry B. II. Title.
ML410.G1527A3   1992
782.25—dc20
    [B]   92–16230
                                                                 CIP
                                                                  MN

Printed in the United States of America
3 4 5 6 7 — 02 01 00

*P*REFACE

I interviewed Bill Gaither for two magazines in the early 1970s, the first time in a dressing room of the Arie Crown Theater at McCormick Place in Chicago. The Bill Gaither Trio—which then included Bill's wife, Gloria, and his brother, Danny—was at the height of its popularity and had sold out the auditorium for two evenings.

It would have been easy for a down-home Hoosier to get used to fame and money and star treatment. But I was struck by Bill's earthiness and normal outlook. The concert was more a worship service than a performance, the audience very much involved.

My next visit with Bill was in the fall of 1974 in Alexandria, Indiana, where he grew up and still lives. The Gaither children—Suzanne, Amy, and Benjy—were youngsters, and the home was warm and intimate.

Nearly two decades later, as we discussed writing this book, Bill and I spent dozens of hours in Alexandria. The family home has been slightly expanded and, because of the growth of its many trees, it is no longer visible from the road. It is also, essentially, an empty nest. Otherwise, the place, and the Gaithers, have not changed. Bill is no longer a rising star, rather now a senior statesman. His influence on Christian music is nearly incalculable. Eager to share his platform, he has catapulted many young musicians to positions of national ministry. He remains a philosophical, roots-oriented man of quick wit and humor whose interest still lies in ministering from the heart and from the gut.

Those who know Bill as a consummate musician will discover here the deep and thoughtful mind behind his art as he speaks out in prose for the first time on a wide range of timely issues. Working with him has been a privilege.

Jerry B. Jenkins

CONTENTS

CHAPTER ONE

MEN, MARY, AND MARTHA

We have this moment to hold in our hands
And to touch as it slips through our fingers like
*   sand.*
Yesterday's gone, and tomorrow may never
*   come,*
But we have this moment, today. *

A rare break in our schedule allowed Gloria and me a few days in Florida. One night on our way to dinner, we noticed a particularly beautiful sky and decided to allow time to watch the sunset from the beach the next evening.

When the time came, however, and I was about to join Gloria on the beach, the phone rang. The call was from a man I had tried to reach early that morning, someone on his way out of the country and whom I needed to talk to about an upcoming appearance.

Despite my trying to hurry things along, the call became involved. In the middle of the conversation, Gloria came in and gave me a look only a wife can give. "What are you doing? Why are you making a call now?"

I covered the phone. "I'm not *making* a call; I'm *taking* a call, and I needed to hear from this guy."

"Well, hurry up. We're going to miss the sunset."

By the time I joined Gloria on the beach, the sun was a sliver of orange on the horizon. It provided just enough light to see her angry shrug. Gloria is generally better than I at saying what she's thinking, and her thoughts were strong: "When are we going to learn this? How old do we have to be and how long do we have to be in this ministry before we realize that some things are more important than others?"

I felt unfairly chastised. "Gloria, I'm sorry, but there was no other time I could talk to the guy."

At that point, she couldn't have cared less if the caller had been George Bush. I was married to this brilliant person who, in my opinion, did not understand the practical things of life. How could my wife of more than twenty-five years be so immature that she could not allow for the busy-ness of my schedule? Some things you have to take care of when you can. My resentment was clear. I did not react well.

Gloria reacted to my reaction, and though we should have known better, it was fifth grade revisited. Suffice it to say, ours was not a pleasant dinner.

Why do I share that story? What value is there in confessing that we—like most married couples—have our squabbles? As you will discover, our relationship is wonderfully frank and we are deeply in love. But I share that story because, first, I came to realize that Gloria was right, and second, because it epitomizes the struggle of many men today.

At first I couldn't believe that Gloria didn't understand how complicated our life was. I try to keep it as uncomplicated as possible, but sometimes I don't have a choice. The problem is that a wife who really cares knows that some things are sacred and should remain sacred. And watching the sunset with the person you love the most in the world is more sacred than any business detail.

As a man this is one of my biggest dilemmas. I spend most of my energy on the practical responsibility of making a living and keeping a business going, just like many of my associates. I ache for them, because, in general, we men have more trouble trying to balance both real worlds: the practical and the ethereal.

Gloria and I happen to be on the extreme ends of the practical-ethereal spectrum. In fact, my longtime friend Bob MacKenzie has called us Peter Practical and Edith Ethereal. To use a biblical metaphor, she's the Mary and I'm the Martha. You know what? Jesus said Mary was right.

Though I was outraged that Gloria couldn't see the much bigger world out there, there was no defense for my position. In reality, hers may be the only truly important world. You don't want to dwell on tragedy, but if something horrible had happened to either of us shortly after that, you can bet the other would have wished we'd spent those moments together on that beautiful shore.

Most of my life is made up of the Mary-Martha dilemma: balancing the practical with those intangible things that will last forever. The Lord knows we have written enough songs about it, trying to call people's attention to what real life is all about.

We Have This Moment, Today

Hold tight to the sound of the music of living,
Happy songs from the laughter of children at play;
Hold my hand as we run through the sweet, fragrant
meadows,
Making memories of what was today.

Tiny voice that I hear is my little girl calling
For Daddy to hear just what she has to say;
My little son running there by the hillside
May never be quite like today.

Tender words, gentle touch, and a good cup of coffee,
And someone who loves me and wants me to stay;
Hold them near while they're here and don't wait for
tomorrow
To look back and wish for today.

Take the blue of the sky and the green of the forest
And the gold and the brown of the freshly mown hay,
Add the pale shades of spring and the circus of autumn,
And weave you a lovely today.

We have this moment to hold in our hands
And to touch as it slips through our fingers like sand.
Yesterday's gone, and tomorrow may never come,
But we have this moment today. *

That's hard to argue with. I can sing it every night and sing it pretty convincingly. Then the phone says, "*I need this moment,*" and the family wants to see the sunset. Sometimes everybody gets the message but me.

*Words by Gloria Gaither. Music by William J. Gaither. Copyright © 1975 by William J. Gaither. International copyright secured. All rights reserved.

I could say, "Hey, I'm doing the best I know how. I'm getting the business of life done." But I know better. Like many other people, I spend too much of my time on the phone. People have car phones, phones in the bathroom, even portable phones they can carry to Little League games so they can not only do their jobs as parents, but also keep up with their businesses. How must it look to a kid who checks to see if Dad saw his big hit, and the old man is on the phone?

There's no getting around it: For the most part, men are in the Martha business and missing a lot of the Mary stuff of life. Ironically, sunsets are important to my work. I have to experience that intangible to be able to express it musically, and, if I theorize without tasting, my creative juices dry up. I somehow grew up feeling a certain amount of guilt if I wasn't working—and working pretty hard—most of the time. I don't just mow the yard; I accomplish something. Fighting not to become a slave to that at the expense of the intangibles is the story of my life. And that's what eats a man's lunch every day. I doubt many men err on the side of the sunsets.

No wonder there's a shortage of male spiritual leadership in homes and churches; we've forgotten what's really important. Some estimate that 75 percent of that spiritual leadership comes from women. Thank God for those women who do come forward, but it's time for us men to assume our responsibility. There's a shortage of male leadership in nearly every level of our society.

What ever happened to the qualities Rudyard Kipling espoused in his famous poem "If"? A framed copy is hanging in my office. My daughter Amy gave it to me to remind me of the qualities I want to espouse as a male in today's society.

If

If you can keep your head when all about you
Are losing theirs and blaming it on you;
If you can trust yourself when all men doubt you,
But make allowance for their doubting too;
If you can wait and not be tired by waiting,
Or being lied about, don't deal in lies,
Or being hated don't give way to hating,
And yet don't look too good, nor talk too wise;

If you can dream—and not make dreams your master,
If you can think—and not make thoughts your aim,
If you can meet with Triumph and Disaster
And treat those two impostors just the same;
If you can bear to hear the truth you've spoken
Twisted by knaves to make a trap for fools,
Or watch the things you gave your life to, broken,
And stoop and build 'em up with worn-out tools;

If you can make one heap of all your winnings
And risk it on one turn of pitch-and-toss,
And lose, and start again at your beginnings,
And never breathe a word about your loss;
If you can force your heart and nerve and sinew
To serve your turn long after they are gone,
And so hold on when there is nothing in you
Except the Will which says to them: "Hold on!"

If you can talk with crowds and keep your virtue,
Or walk with Kings—nor lose the common touch,
If neither foes nor loving friends can hurt you,
If all men count with you, but none too much;
If you can fill the unforgiving minute
With sixty seconds' worth of distance run,

Yours is the Earth and everything that's in it,
*And—which is more—you'll be a Man, my son!**

To me the most significant line in that poem is this: "If you can meet with Triumph and Disaster and treat those two impostors just the same. . . ." What was he saying? In a most graceful, understated way, he was profound. *Both* triumph and disaster are impostors! Winning and losing are not always what they seem, a jarring thought to men who were raised to win at all costs.

We've all heard the adages "Winning isn't everything; it's the only thing" and "Show me a good loser and I'll show you a loser." Even as Christians we are much more comfortable winning than losing. You can see it in our emphasis on the size of our churches. Is a bigger church really more significant? Some of the most significant work for the kingdom is properly being done in small congregations. Yet pastors suffer with the comparisons. I'm not saying smaller is spiritual and bigger isn't. But we need to get our perspectives and our priorities straight. We're exclusive, and proud of it, because we are on the winning side. But we've lost sight of what it took to win. For us to live, Jesus had to die. For us to be rich, we must give. To be honored, we must be humble. To be leaders, we must serve.

As men, we are confused about the paradoxes of winning and losing. Rather than dealing with that confusion and working toward a solution, we have abdicated our leadership roles, gone into our success-oriented cocoons, and gone about the business of winning. Prospering. Achieving. But as Kipling implied, winning and losing

*Rudyard Kipling (1865–1936). Public Domain.

aren't that different. Jesus showed us that sometimes losing *is* winning. And winning is losing.

You should have seen my first idea for the title of this
book. I wanted to call it: *Sometimes We Win, Sometimes
We Lose, Sometimes We Get Rained Out, But Most of the
Time We Don't Know the Difference Until Later!* What we
think is a tremendous victory now may turn out to be the
worst thing that ever happened to us. What we think is a
horrible loss today may turn out to be the best thing that
ever happened to us. That's why winning and losing, triumph and disaster, are impostors. Winning at all costs has
turned us men (and some women) into Marthas, when
what we need are more Marys.

If you're like me, you meet a man, and within two
minutes of getting acquainted you get around to asking,
"What do you do for a living?" What makes us like that?
We care where he's from or who he's related to, but we
tend to believe a man's identity is the same thing as how
he makes his living. Most men are proud to tell you what
they do because that's how they define themselves too. In
our heads we start ranking each other, guessing at in-
comes and lifestyles. It's the nature of men. We're defined
by what we do and we're measured by how well we do it.
Are you a senior partner, or just an associate? Are you with
a company that's in trouble, or are you with the leading
firm in your field?

Why do we do that? I think it was bred into us from
the time we first bragged to our friends, "My dad can beat
up your dad. My dog's faster than your dog. Our house is
bigger than your house." I used to come in from playing
tennis when Benjy was little, and the first thing he would
ask was "Did you win, Dad?" I didn't teach him that. (If
you saw me play tennis, you'd know I didn't teach him to

ask that!) It's somehow naturally important to us how we and our parents do in competition, and it seems more prevalent among males than females, especially as we grow up. We're more subtle about it now, but we still compare, don't we?

It's insidious when you think about it, because this emphasis on winning makes everything else seem like losing. Take an Olympic sprinter who is better than all other sprinters in the world but one. He may go two or three years without losing a race, then finish second to the world record holder by three one-hundredths of a second. He wins a silver medal and comes within an eyelash of a record and the gold medal himself, but a day later no one knows his name. He's not the one on the Wheaties box with the multi-million dollar deals. Because he was second by a margin that only high-tech electronic equipment could measure, he lost.

I love to watch sports. At its best it is a picture of life. A team may lose, but in losing learn something or gain maturity that allows them to win a championship in the end. Another team may win an otherwise meaningless game, but lose a key player to injury that costs them success in the long run. Or they may become arrogant and overconfident and lose that crucial chemistry that once set them apart.

What we men need to see is that winning and losing are not all that important in the end. The crucial issue is who we are, what we are, and what we were called to do on this earth. Is a missionary who has worked for decades in a hard-scrabble desert with one or two converts a loser? Is he a success or a failure? It depends on who's keeping score.

That's why it's vital not to react too quickly to circumstances in life, to have the patience to look at a tough circumstance long enough to see how it is going to affect us in God's long-range plan for our lives.

Permit me another sports analogy. It's hard for a pro quarterback to stay in the pocket—like all the great coaches want their field leaders to do—when the blocking has broken down and a 280-pound bruiser is charging right at him. The occasional young, athletic quarterback can scramble, but the majority of your Hall of Famers hang in there and take it. They don't panic; they stay in the pocket.

That example has been helpful to me over the years. There have been times when I have done what I felt God told me to do, and yet life came charging at me in a 280-pound package, ready to cream me. I wanted to scramble for the sidelines. When I stayed in the pocket and kept doing what I was supposed to be doing, the day eventually came when I saw the whys and wherefores. And even if I haven't seen them yet, I know I will someday. Every time we think we come to the end of something, we may be at the beginning of something else without knowing it. That's why Jesus talks in terms of comparing Himself to the Alpha and the Omega, the beginning and the end. What did He mean? He meant both. We don't know the difference. What we think is the end may be the beginning, and vice versa.

Staying in the pocket characterizes any man who lasts in spite of the uncertainties of life. Not knowing whether that half-minute play will result in success or failure should make us want to get the pass off, take the hit, and see what God has in mind for the game as a whole.

If our identity is wrapped up in winning and losing, we're going to be up and down many times in our lives.

When we are in one of those slumps, we are the most vulnerable to doing something we'll regret.

God is looking for men He can trust, men who have real integrity, men who will prioritize their lives in such a way that loving "the Lord your God with all your heart" is number one and that loving their wives, children, and neighbors is next. My daughter Suzanne and her husband, Barry Jennings, wrote a song that perfectly reflects that sentiment. I want to be one of those men.

A Few Good Men

What this dying world could use is a willing man of God
Who dares to go against the grain and work without
applause,
A man who'll raise the sword of faith, protecting what is
pure,
Whose love is tough and gentle, a man whose word is
sure.

God doesn't need an orator who knows just what to say.
He doesn't need authorities to reason Him away.
He doesn't need an army to guarantee a win;
He just needs a few good men.

Men full of compassion who laugh and love and cry,
Men who'll face eternity and aren't afraid to die;
Men who'll fight for freedom and honor once again,
He just needs a few good men.

He calls the broken derelict whose life has been renewed,
He calls the one who has the strength to stand up for the
truth.

Enlistment lines are open, and He wants you to come in:
He just needs a few good men. *

It's tragic that there are men who call themselves
Christians who are not honorable in their business deal-
ings. Occasionally someone will say, "You'd better be
careful when you deal with him." Why should that be nec-
essary in the Christian community?

On the other hand, you sometimes hear someone say
simply, "He's a good man; you can trust him."

A man can't buy a reputation like that.

*Words by Suzanne Gaither Jennings. Music by Barry Jennings. Copy-
right © 1990 by Townsend and Warbucks Music. All rights reserved. International copyright secured. Used by permission.

CHAPTER TWO

THE MEASURE OF A GOOD MAN

*A good name is to be chosen rather than great
  riches,
Loving favor rather than silver and gold.*
                                        —Proverbs 22:1

---

*M*y son Benjy, about to leave for an inner-city ministry for the summer between college terms, was doing some yard work with me. He looked around our fifteen acres with its stream, its trees, its rolling grass. "This place is beautiful," he said. "How did you get it?"

Kids tend to take things for granted until they're about to leave or lose them. "I thought you'd never ask," I said, and I told Benjy the story of our property.

Gloria and I had been married a couple of years and had only one child, Suzanne. We were teaching school in Alexandria, Indiana, where I had grown up, and we wanted a piece of land where we could build a house. I noticed the parcel south of town where cattle grazed, and I learned it belonged to a ninety-two-year-old retired banker named Mr. Yule. He owned a lot of land in the area, and the word was he would sell none of it. He gave the same speech to everyone who inquired. "I promised the farmers they could use it for their cattle."

Gloria and I visited him at the bank, cute little Suzanne in tow, bonnet in place. We found the elderly gent in an office, reading his *Wall Street Journal*. Although he was retired he spent a couple of hours each morning in his office. He looked at us over the top of his bifocals.

I introduced myself and my family and told him we were interested in a piece of his land. "Not selling," he said pleasantly. "Promised it to a farmer for grazing."

"I know, but we teach school here and thought maybe you'd be interested in selling it to someone planning to settle in the area."

He pursed his lips and stared at me. "What'd you say your name was?"

"Gaither. Bill Gaither."

"Hmm. Any relation to Grover Gaither?"

"Yes sir. He was my granddad."

Mr. Yule put down his paper and removed his glasses. "Interesting. Grover Gaither was the best worker I ever had on my farm. Full day's work for a day's pay. So honest. What'd you say you wanted?"

I told him again.

"Let me do some thinking on it, then come back and see me."

I came back within the week, and Mr. Yule told me he had had the property appraised. I held my breath. "How does thirty-eight hundred sound? Would that be okay?"

If that was per acre, I would have to come up with

nearly sixty thousand dollars! "Thirty-eight hundred?" I repeated.

"Yup. Fifteen acres for thirty-eight hundred."

I knew it had to be worth at least three times that. I readily accepted.

Nearly three decades later, my son and I strolled that beautiful, lush property that had once been pasture land. "Benjy," I said, "you've had this wonderful place to grow up through nothing that you've done, but because of the good name of a great-granddad you never met."

Grover Gaither is a man I'll never forget. He had a great sense of humor. The night before he died, he told jokes and laughed so hard he cried. The next day, out in the fields on his tractor, he died of a heart attack. I remember thinking, *What a wonderful way that must have been to go home and meet the Lord, even though personally there is a lot of pain for us because we loved him so.*

At his funeral my granddad was praised for his compassion, his ability to forgive, his strength, his tenderness, and his generosity. He had been a man of gentle leadership, of integrity. He had been a simple farmer, but his demeanor and lifestyle marked him with greatness. People kept coming up to me and saying, "Your grandfather was a good man."

A good man. That's a wonderful phrase that has been lost in our culture. That's the kind of legacy I want to leave my children. No one has to praise my talents, abilities, or achievements. I will die a happy man if I believe people viewed me as a good man who truly loved the Lord, especially in an age when integrity is so scarce.

With my children I've found that integrity is not something I can teach; it's something I have to model. Kids can be pretty tough evaluators. Integrity means following through on my commitments, honoring an engagement even if I'm sick—unless I can't get out of bed.

Some mistakenly believe there are levels or degrees of integrity. In truth, integrity is black or white. It's really a yes or a no. My good friend Robert Nicholson was like that. When he was president of Anderson College and we board members were ready to vote on something, I remember his saying, "Before you vote, you need to know of this one possibility that might change the whole picture."

The chances of that one thing's happening may have been one in a thousand, but he wanted to make sure that everybody had all the information before deciding. That's truth and honesty. That's modeling integrity.

A person's reputation—his honor—is worth more than wealth and possessions. I thank God for the kind of home I grew up in, for my parents and grandparents and aunts and uncles, for the models of integrity I enjoyed during my formative years.

There is a lifestyle consistent with what God wants and expects from His children. The world ought to see that we are different. We ought to be good examples to those who know us. But don't misunderstand me: I'm not there yet either. I'm still working on it. Am I preaching some kind of perfection? I'd better not be, because that would eliminate me too. My desire is to be worthy of the kind of investment others have made in my life by being a man of God—for my wife, for my children, for my church, for my business associates, and for my community.

We all need a little breathing room, space to grow and develop our weaker areas. Otherwise, none of us will make it. So, again, I'm not talking about perfection, some kind of "superman." I'm talking about commitment to an ideal, striving, working. That kind of life doesn't earn salvation. No kind of life earns salvation. Only death does that, and we needed Someone else to do that for us. Striving toward holiness does not earn salvation, but salvation should result in a lifestyle that is honoring to the price He paid for our salvation. Once one has truly experienced grace and forgiveness, then I believe he is overwhelmed with an incredible gratitude. Out of gratitude, then, one responds to the ultimate gift from God.

I realize I'm walking a fine line between grace and a call to right living, but I'm certainly not anti-grace. I'm not even saying that we've been too kind and that there's been cheap grace. At the same time, we need to be men of our word. We've made promises. Kids are watching. Educators still say kids learn more by watching than by hearing. When I look back on my career as a teacher and as a student, my favorite teachers were those who were something or did something, rather than those who just said something. I learned discipline, not from any book, but from watching a college professor who had very few discipline problems.

There is no such thing as perfection here on earth. There is no perfect church, no perfect pastor, no perfect marriage, no perfect business, no perfect college, no perfect city, no perfect ball team. Every human group is made up of individuals who are imperfect at their cores. The older you get, the shorter will become your list of heroes.

I'm thankful for those in my life who have remained giants, not because of their perfection, but because of their integrity and humility and a relentless pursuit of the ultimate model of our Lord. They have certainly been my models.

Truly humble men of integrity, models for us and our children, are not born. They're reborn. A man who doesn't know his heavenly Father is going to be forever insecure. A grown man often exhibits insecurities. Why? Because he's never come to the heavenly Father with what Paul calls in 2 Corinthians 7:9–10 a godly sorrow:

> Now I rejoice, not that you were made sorry, but that your sorrow led to repentance. For you were made sorry in a godly manner, that you might suffer loss from us in nothing. For godly sorrow produces repentance leading to salvation, not to be regretted; but the sorrow of the world produces death.

Repentance is an old-fashioned word, but it's also a great psychological principle. It means we're genuinely sorry because we have grieved the heart of God. Worldly sorrow, Paul says, brings death. A real man understands the difference.

Repentance and godly sorrow that lead to salvation also lead to a changed life. That's good news for people from dysfunctional families, the children of physical and sexual abusers, people who chronically break relationships, alcoholics, drug addicts. There's enough grace at the foot of the cross for you to be the first Johnson or Smith or Jones or Gaither in generations to break the cycle of devastation in your family tree. You can be the one who says, "As for me and my house, we will serve the Lord. And we're going to have a whole, healthy, repentant, godly sorrowful man who knows Jesus and will lead the way. The alcoholism, the devastation, the tragic failure ends here."

How else do we become good men? First, we have to

admit we don't know all the answers. Something in our nature makes us bad at this. Many women, as soon as they realize they are in trouble, look for help. They ask directions; they seek advice; they consult with friends; they do things in groups. We men often want to do it all ourselves. I won't ask for directions until we're utterly lost and fifty miles from the right path. I'd sooner mess up a project than admit I need help. I don't even read directions. I can be going down for the third time in my life, and if someone asks how I'm doing, I'll say, "Fine, great, fantastic." A real man is one honest enough to say, "If you really want to know, I'm hurting."

Some years ago I called Bob Reardon, an ex-president of Anderson College and one of those mentor-models in my life. I was finally at a point where I knew I needed help. I asked if he had a few minutes. I went to see him around nine at night and blubbered for about three hours. I was embarrassed, but he was a big enough man to sit and listen, to not judge, to laugh and cry and pray with me and help me put my problems in perspective, all because I admitted I needed help.

Did that make me less of a man? Not at all.

A book that has had a tremendous impact on my life is *Healing the Masculine Soul* by Dr. Gordon Dalbey (Word, 1988), which discusses the whole business of the independent nature of men. Spiritual faith, Dalbey says, is considered by many men a most personal matter, something of which they rarely speak. Most often faith is seen as a woman's prerogative because of a "lack of independence and self-assurance that does not coincide with [a man's] macho self-image." Dalbey goes on to say, "There is a tear in the masculine soul," which he describes as a wound, a gaping hole that "leads to a profound insecurity."

German psychologist Alexander Mitscherlich wrote that "society has torn the soul of the male, and into this tear demons have fled. Demons of insecurity, selfishness, and despair." If you read your daily newspaper, you know the truth of that statement.

How can we be real men in a society like ours? We must follow the leads of those few men who have preceded us with grace and humility—those few who developed and exhibited a healthy respect for other people and what they do. Those men who never quit learning, who remained students of life. Those men who discovered the difference between winning and losing and treated both those impostors the same. Those who were men of their word, who honored their commitments and didn't break their vows. Those who were gracious and forgiving, understanding that "but for the grace of God, there go I."

A good man is a man who has 1 Corinthians 13 type love. He is vulnerable. Does he eat quiche? Does he cry? Is he tender? I think so. Let me tell you of the good men, besides my grandfather and Bob Reardon, who have influenced me. There are many more than I can cover here, but as you read of these men and why they were so important to me, perhaps you'll wonder as I often do, who will fill their shoes in the next generation? If they influenced me, will I influence anyone? And will the ones I influence pass on a worthy legacy, should God tarry? It's an ominous question, one we should ask ourselves daily.

CHAPTER THREE

WHO'S GOING TO FILL THEIR SHOES?

*By faith Noah, being divinely warned of things
not yet seen, moved with godly fear, prepared
an ark for the saving of his household, by
which he condemned the world and became
heir of the righteousness which is according to
faith.*

—Hebrews 11:7

*P*eople are watching us whether we want to admit it or not. If you don't believe it, look at your own household. The kids keep score. We are either a positive or a negative influence on others. I'm not necessarily trying to make a case for modeling; I'm trying to make a case for integrity. As followers of Christ, our goal should be to point others to Him.

No man is an island. When we fail, we don't fall alone. We always take impressionable young minds and souls with us. When our basic character begins to crumble, when our integrity is called into question, little is left to build upon.

Anybody can make a mistake, but the foundation of

what we're all about, the seed of our being, must be regenerated by the blood of Christ. Then we have an obligation to let Him live through us so we can represent Him with honor. In this day when young people are disillusioned, thank God there are those we can point to and say, "He has done some things right."

We men have not taken our God-given responsibility to pick up the towel and basin and wash feet as true servant-leaders in our own homes. If we continue to allow generations to come and go with a lack of male leadership, we're going to reap serious consequences; some have already begun. If you think we're in trouble now, imagine one or two generations from now. We have only begun to see the social ills that will follow.

One of the biggest causes of drug and alcohol abuse may be that we men feel intimidated, short-changed, and threatened in our society. Some feel they have not received a fair shake, which can cause depression. That depression can lead to substance abuse and crime. Then, some who feel they cannot live honestly at an economic level they feel they deserve, will do so dishonestly.

Too many husbands and fathers have had no positive role models and have no idea how to be tender, how to love their wives, how to do anything but lash out when things don't go their way. They use their physical superiority and power to intimidate and get what they want.

The lack of good role models in the home can lead to dysfunction, which we hear a lot about today. The word *dysfunctional* describes people who have not learned and grown from the way they were raised, but rather have found themselves paralyzed by it.

Those who say they can't do anything about it run the risk of making the work of Christ a joke. Rather than claiming the power of the resurrected Christ to stop the legacy of alcoholism and drug addiction, wife beating, child and sexual abuse, the victims stay mired in a cycle of sin. Fortunately, there are now many good Christian psychologists to aid these people in dealing with their pasts and breaking the cycles of sin.

It's a humbling thing to talk about godly leadership, that leadership prized by God. I've said that I don't put myself in the category of those who have arrived— perhaps no one has arrived, not even the men I will cite from my own history. But like it or not, regardless of where we stand in this area of spiritual maturity, we are models for good or bad in our own homes, if nowhere else.

In Scripture there are many models of leadership, and not one of them was perfect—except Jesus Christ Himself, of course. Noah, Gideon, Joshua, and David are among my favorites. Despite their failings and shortcomings, they learned from them and had the courage to follow God against all odds. They started the pursuit to a higher calling. Noah had the dogged faith to defy the world in the face of ridicule and faithlessness over *centuries* of obedience to God.

Gideon's faith was certainly not in numbers. He was committed to God, believing against all logic that the Commander of the universe would carry his tiny band of warriors to victory against enemy hordes.

Joshua followed a call to serve God in sincerity and truth, again, going against peer pressure and tremendous odds.

David, in spite of his gross sin, returned to contriteness that made him desire to be a man after God's own heart.

Obviously, I can write only from a male perspective.

The men in my life who taught me the most are men who may not have realized they were teaching me anything. They didn't use lectures or lessons. Their methods were their lives. Occasionally one, like my Uncle Jesse, would use a well-worded sentence to prove to me that he cared and that he was thinking about me and my values, my future, my character.

One time I was angry over something that had happened in our church, and I spouted off about it. Uncle Jesse calmed me by saying simply, "Bill, you know, you can be right and still be wrong." How true. I may have been right in my opinion, right in my convictions, right in my judgment about the issue. But I was surely wrong about how I expressed it and tried to change it. I'm grateful for an uncle who cared about me enough to have the courage to tell me the truth, gently but firmly.

Uncle Jesse was known as the man in our church you could call on to pray if you had a need. People took him seriously and treated him with respect because of his close walk with the Lord. Was he perfect? No. I knew him as a man of God, but also as a man who was a lot of fun and was able to make jokes at his own expense. He helped me learn that being a real man did not necessarily mean being tall, dark, and handsome or being able to bend steel rods in your bare hands.

I've been blessed by other strong men in my life. After my Granddad Grover came my own father, of course, a man of quiet strength, solid as a rock. Then, when I became the first kid in our family to go to college and went to what is now Anderson University, I met Robert Nicholson. He was a giant of a man who, upon closer inspection as I grew older, was one of those rare men who remains a giant. I studied under him, and years later he became president of Anderson. Dr. Nicholson was a good professor, not so much because of what he said, as because of who he was, what he did, and how he did it. He could have fun in the classroom and still impart values and knowledge. You look at a man like that during an impressionable stage in your life, and you say, "I want to be like that." He had fun, but he was serious about life. He was a man to emulate, a man whose traits were worth copying. When I eventually became a junior high and then high school teacher, I discovered I had unconsciously patterned many of my methods after Dr. Nicholson. More importantly, my character had been enriched. To see him in times of crisis—when integrity really counted—was to see him as a servant. He talked about servanthood, and he modeled it. He was a wonderful example.

Dr. Eugene Stowe, a minister in the Church of the Nazarene who later became general superintendent of the denomination, had an air about him of sophistication and brilliance, of love and compassion. I would see him in the pulpit and think, *I'd like to be like that man.*

Dr. Karl Kardatzke, another professor of mine, was one of the first Christians to talk about psychology and family issues back when that wasn't popular. Some today believe you're tampering with the gospel if you apply psychology to it, but back then that feeling was even more widespread. I had Dr. Kardatzke for adolescent psychology. He was a great teacher, but one of my fondest recollections was seeing him once outside of class. At a midweek prayer meeting at the old Park Place Church, I saw him sitting in his folding chair, tilted back to the wall as we sang "The Old Rugged Cross." When we got to the chorus, "So, I'll cherish the old rugged cross," I saw tears streaming down his cheeks, this sophisticated man of letters, an accomplished educator with a string of degrees, weeping at the thought of what Jesus had done for him. What a precious memory!

I knew then that real men, even learned men, could care deeply about their faith. A few weeks later Dr. Kardatzke was diagnosed with terminal cancer. I heard that as he lay dying, he said to his wife, "Well, Tip, it's been a great life with you. Let's thank God for forty-seven years together."

Without realizing it, he had spoken volumes to me. He had lived and died without regret—maybe one of the strongest testimonies of the strength of a man's character and the power of his faith. He went to be with the Lord as a real man. That was a role model, the kind of man a young person doesn't forget. Who's going to fill his shoes? Are we raising a generation of young people who can develop that kind of character and sensitivity, or have we sold the entire lot down the river of dysfunction, me-first attitudes, materialism, acquisition, and looking out for number one?

I have hope when I look at some of our young people today. There *are* some good folks around, quietly doing significant things. They may not want to be highly visible. They have names few would recognize, but they will be known in heaven one day. Our company controller, Dan Lacy, can be a hard-nosed businessman, just the way he needs to be and the way we want him to be. But on Sunday mornings he's surrounded in church by a swarm of eager kindergartners. And he's not just helping out; he's teaching just as he has for years. Here is a guy giving up his seat in the worship service to serve children. The biggest heroes in our congregations may not be in public leadership, but rather people like Dan, willing to model servanthood. The world might ignore Dan's devotion, but it's time we believers started recognizing the hidden heroes of the kingdom, not to stroke their egos, but to encourage others to emulate them.

One of the most Christlike people I know is a man in his early thirties named Randy Sigler. He's in charge of our buildings and grounds. Few know him, but those who do are influenced by him in spite of his youth and lack of visibility. He's simply quiet and humbly spiritual.

What does it take to be a man like that? More than your own generating plant, that's for sure. God has to be in those men, making them good and strong, preparing their lives to get the attention of the next generation.

In our natural selves we might run from the responsibility of being models. But whether I like it or not, I am a model in my home and, because I'm the owner, I'm a model in my business as well. What does that mean for me? In a practical sense, I've learned the hard way that words can be hurtful. Thinking of others before speaking is a daily learned behavior, not unlike the daily renewing of the mind Paul speaks of in Romans.

I'm not hanging out any sign that says I'm a role model, and, if anyone did, I'd burn it. But many people are looked to for leadership whether or not they seek such a calling. I doubt Billy Graham ever would have volunteered to be the model for the evangelical community—in fact I've read that the loss of his privacy has been one of the greatest sacrifices of his life.

I've had men ask me how we can model spiritual leadership in our homes. I am married to a lady who is very verbal, not only on spiritual matters, but on everything from the way the schools are run to how we do things around the house. Her views and her ability to articulate them are among the many things I love so much about her. They give her an edge on some of our day-to-day family needs. But I still have a spiritual responsibility to lead my family. Sometimes crises bring out more of my strengths. I think I can put things in perspective pretty well, find a spiritual dimension to the problem, and take the opportunity to bring God into the mix. But it takes both of us working together to keep our family healthy and happy. I believe parents (particularly fathers) should seize the opportunity when they see a spiritual "opening in the line" and say, in essence, "Give me the ball and see if I know where to go with this one." I'm trying to do better in bringing out spiritual dimensions on a day-to-day basis, not letting Gloria shoulder all the responsibility. But to be honest with you, neither of us would have made it as a parent without the other.

As a spiritual leader in my home, when I detected a need I tried to step in and deal with it. For instance, we didn't gloss over the issue of divorce when it touched those around us. We've used such incidents to point out to our kids the importance of right choices early in life, of following through on commitments in spite of all odds, of building a family on a biblical foundation. As painful as it is, we've tried to point out to the kids that someone's divorce does not put an end to their spiritual pilgrimage. In other words, we can learn from both positive and negative experiences in life.

Not every day is there a spiritual trauma that needs my direction. One of Gloria's strengths—and she has written extensively on this—is finding the spiritual in the mundane, everyday things of life. She's better at that than I am. Of course, she's no slouch when it comes to crises either, but it's important for husbands and wives to know each other's strengths so they can fill their respective roles effectively.

Sad to say, but I think it's true: Women are generally more principled than men and less quick to bail out of problems. We men could learn something from our wives about that. Men are more collegial by nature and sometimes more willing to compromise for the sake of what they see as the bigger picture. A woman will more likely say, "If it isn't just so, don't do it." My word to the man struggling with these differences is: "Thank God for the struggle." Gloria and I have learned to complement each other. She has learned that things are not always as cut and dried as they seem at first. She has taught me to stand firm at times when I might otherwise have given in. We've learned from each other never to give up.

Thank God for the many women who have modeled Christian leadership. Some of the great missionaries in history were and are women: Think of Amy Carmichael, Elisabeth Elliot, Mother Teresa. These women were called to fill the gap, and they responded. I am thankful. There's nothing wrong with a woman's taking a leadership position, but there seems to be a lack of godly male leadership just now. This is not a chauvinistic statement. There should be no power or privilege associated with leadership the way God designed it and Jesus modeled it. Humility, meekness, gentleness, kindness, servanthood, putting others first, loving our spouses as Christ loved the church—these are the characteristics of true leadership. Where are the men who will humble themselves to be true, committed, dependable servant-leaders?

I get a kick out of watching Mother Teresa when the media crowds around her and tries to capture her good deeds on camera. Often you see a look of resigned exasperation in her eyes when she looks to the intruders, as if to say, "What are you doing? Please let me get on with what I am supposed to do."

The great Dutch stateswoman and Nazi death camp survivor Corrie ten Boom was a model of humility to me. She and her traveling companion came to our annual Praise Gathering one year, and they arrived several days in advance so she could be settled before she had to speak. Corrie was powerful and effective in her presence and her presentation. When we went to check her out of her hotel and see her on her way at the end of the week, she apologized for the bill. "I hope we didn't eat too much," she said. "We occasionally had milk and crackers."

I was so stunned at the minuscule bill for a week that I nearly laughed. I wish some of the Christian artists I know could learn from Corrie. "If that's too much," she added, "I'll be happy to pay it."

Here's this saint who came into tremendous celebrity at age seventy-five, and for the last ten years of her life had a press corps following her nearly everywhere she went. She "stayed in the pocket," continuing to do what God called her to do. She never became impressed with herself. She was the same woman known worldwide that she had been when no one knew her name.

It's tough to convince a young person in our business that one day the flashbulbs will quit flashing. If your whole identity is wrapped up in your voice or your talent or in the reaction of the crowd, someday school's going to be out for you. We need more men to model humility the way some of these great saintly women have.

Who's going to fill the shoes of those men who went before me, of these women who exhibited the leadership qualities of Christ? The matter of a legacy should be a real driving force for men. Every man in the world must ask himself, "What am I leaving? What good can be said about me? At my funeral, will they say I was good to my wife, kind to animals, anything?"

When I'm dead and gone I don't know what my kids will say about the business I've been involved in. I don't know what they'll say about all the people we've sung to or sold records to or about all the awards we've received. But I'm serious when I say that I hope they'll remember their dad as an honest man who loved Jesus with all his heart and who pursued a Christlike lifestyle every day.

But even when I fail, the beautiful thing about the body of Christ is that the family of God is the one place where failure is not terminal.

Something Beautiful

If there ever were dreams that were lofty and noble,
They were my dreams at the start;
And the hopes for life's best were the hopes that I
harbored
Down deep in my heart.

But my dreams turned to ashes, my castles all crumbled,
My fortune turned to loss,
So I wrapped it all in the rags of my life,
And laid it at the cross!

Something beautiful, something good;
All my confusion, He understood;
All I had to offer Him was brokenness and strife,
But He made something beautiful of my life. *

That's the kind of business God's in. Isn't that good news? So when you hear me ask who will fill the shoes of the role models who have gone before, look in the mirror. In your own unique way, visible or invisible, known or unknown, it could be you. Hang in there. Keep an eternal perspective. We don't always get paid at the end of the day. The trick is to make magic of the routine. We create our own excitement. I love friends who keep me accountable, who will pull me up rather than drag me down. Find something to give yourself to, a Sunday school class, a boys club, somewhere to serve. Be a real child of God who has enough of your basic character together so that in times of crisis you can be counted on. There are so few people like that, men and women who are there and who are solid when we need them.

May we never quit striving for this ideal. Since I was nineteen years old, I've wanted to be a man of God, and regardless of where I am on the journey now, it's sure been worth the trip.

I'm not what I want to be, and I'm not what I'm gonna be, but thank God I'm not what I was!*

---

*From "I'm Not What I Want to Be." Words by Gloria Gaither. Music by William J. Gaither and Gary S. Paxton. Copyright © 1978 by William J. Gaither (ASCAP) and Christian Grit Music Press (ASCAP). International copyright secured. All rights reserved.

CHAPTER FOUR

WHAT I WAS

I'm so glad I'm a part of the family of God!
I've been washed in the fountain, cleansed by
His blood.
Joint heirs with Jesus as we travel this sod,
For I'm part of the family, the family of God. *

I grew up in the warm, loving family of a skilled toolmaker and a skilled homemaker. We attended the Nazarene Church in Alexandria, Indiana (population 6,000—it hasn't changed by ten in the last forty years!), where I loved the music from as early as I can remember. My brother and sister and I enjoyed listening to the great southern gospel quartets on the radio and even got to some of their concerts when they sang anywhere close to us.

Besides being up at the crack of dawn every morning

with my brother, Danny, to milk the cows, I took piano lessons, sang with Danny and my sister, Mary Ann, sang in musicals at school, played and sang at church, and set my sights on a career as a musician. My dream was to play or sing or both with a well-known gospel group. When my voice changed and I got a standing ovation at the high school variety show for my solo of "Ol' Man River," I thought, *Boy, I'm good*. I enjoyed being in front of a crowd, and I dreamed of traveling and performing with the heroes of my youth. Mostly I wanted to be on stage.

As soon as I graduated from high school in 1954, I went after my dream. I joined a group of young guys in a quartet called The Pathfinders. We eventually migrated to the Columbus, Ohio, area where we landed a daily fifteen-minute radio show. It was sponsored by Pennington Bread on WRFD Radio in Worthington, and we taped the program early in the morning to be aired at noon. We hoped our show would get people to invite us to their churches.

We thought we were in the big leagues when the southern quartets came through because we got to share the stage with greats like the Blackwood Brothers and the Statesmen. To be truthful, I thought I was charming, funny, fantastic, and a great singer. I fully expected one of those groups to discover me. I was sure they'd fire whoever they needed to, to make room for me. I was nineteen and I was ready.

We hustled. We worked hard. And mostly, we starved. It was appropriate that we were sponsored by a bread company because I remember many days subsisting on nothing but toast and coffee. After many months a sense of foreboding set in when we all realized—and I especially—that it wasn't happening for us. Something was missing. We didn't have the magic it took to make it, and there was no future for us.

It came to a head for me one afternoon at the county fairgrounds in Van Wert, Ohio, when we heard how few tickets had been sold for our concert in the 4-H building that night. Sales were so thin that if I had been less stunned I might have laughed. I needed to be alone, so I made my way out to behind the auditorium and cried bitter tears.

I'd had disappointments in my life—from being seventh man on our school basketball team and hardly ever getting to play to losing a girlfriend or two after thinking they would be the loves of my life—but this was devastating. It wasn't just the small crowd we expected that night. It was the end for me, and I knew it.

For the first time in my life I had to stare my dream in the face and realize that I was about to wake up. I didn't have it. My vocal skills and my keyboard skills were not good enough for me to make it in the music business, and that was that. "God," I prayed, "there has to be more to life than this." I committed myself to do whatever He wanted, even though I had no idea what that was. I told Him, "I don't know what I'm going to do, but I'm not going to do this anymore." Sometimes you have to make a decision, not even knowing the ramifications.

That was deeply painful for a nineteen year old. I was faced with the prospect of hanging my dream in the closet. Besides the disappointment, I had to ask myself, "William, what are you going to do to make a living?" I came from a long line of men skilled with their hands, who earned their wages in the factories. But that was not where my skills or interests lay.

Sad to say, that afternoon in Van Wert I had one of my

first real encounters with God. I was a believer, but my spiritual experiences had been mostly emotional. I had been as sincere as a young teen could be, and I had worn a path to the altar in our church every time a new evangelist had come to town. But nothing ever seemed to change my behavior. Even my goals in music had been more to make a living at what I enjoyed than to have any ministry. I had very little in the way of a philosophical or theological background. I just wanted to get on with my life and make a living.

But at the lowest point in my young existence, I had nowhere to turn. I was a failure, my hopes shattered, and all I could express to God was that if music was not what He wanted for me, I was willing to give it up. It wounded me, but I did it. I realized I was empty and how little I had to offer. Then and there I told the Lord, "I want to be totally Yours." In my mind, that meant my musical career was over.

The next morning I told the rest of the guys, "I'm going home." They tried to talk me out of it. They said things were just starting to come together, but I had been hearing that for months. I would not be dissuaded.

Disappointed and disillusioned I came back home and got a job at Cox's, the local supermarket. The only other things I enjoyed and had some academic success at were English and literature, so I enrolled at Taylor University and commuted every day to Upland, Indiana. There would be no southern quartet music at Taylor, because that style of gospel was considered an illegitimate art form in colleges back then. But during the drive every morning I tuned in fifty-thousand-watt WOWL and listened to the Weatherford Quartet's morning show, and that was the only thing that made that year at Taylor bearable. I didn't like the academic part of it. I disliked the long drive. I didn't like that I didn't understand most of my classes and had to work hard just to make C's.

In the middle of all that, what could have been the break of a lifetime came right to my doorstep. One day Earl Weatherford and his wife stopped by and offered me a job in their group. They had heard me play and thought I was what they needed at the keyboards. They offered me a lot more money than I had been making to travel with them. "Do I want a job? Of course! I'd love to do that." I told them I would talk to my parents and call them.

My dad, who was always gentle and soft-spoken, rarely said no. But now he did. "You've started at Taylor and you'll finish out this year." I knew that if he felt that strongly, there had to be a reason. I would not argue or beg. My parents were hard-working Germans with a secure foundation, and I'm sure Dad doubted the stability of the situation I had been offered. He and Mom had seen me struggle to make ends meet for a year with my own group, and what he really wanted was for his son to get a college education.

I didn't know it then, of course, just as I didn't know how pivotal the experience in Van Wert had been, but my dad's advice was some of the best I ever received. Though I was again deeply disappointed, I had already resigned myself to the fact that music was not in my future. I knew that by the time my freshman year had ended, the Weatherfords would have hired someone else. And there were no other opportunities out there like that.

For my sophomore year I transferred to Anderson College, which was fifteen miles closer and where I knew more of the students. For some reason, maybe because I finally had made peace with myself about my potential in music, things started to gel for me. I formed a nucleus of friends there and began to understand what studying was all about. I never became a great student outside my own areas of interest, but I was able to make B's and C's when I applied myself. I got involved in the college choir, minored in music, majored in English, and decided to go after a teaching degree. I knew I would enjoy that, and the academic atmosphere became exciting to me as it never had before.

I got together with my brother, Danny, and my sister, Mary Ann, and on weekends we sang in area churches and civic clubs as the first Gaither Trio. By my junior year we were getting so many requests that I was able to quit my job at Cox's and pay my way through school with the part-time singing work. I didn't allow myself to rekindle the dream, because I knew I was not good enough. The reason so many churches asked us back was because of something I had nothing to do with. Something was happening spiritually when we sang, and all we were singing was material written by others. If there was a singer in the family, it was Danny, who had a strong, clear voice that melted people's hearts. Mary Ann and I blended well with him, and I played the keyboards and emceed. Ironically, we started getting some better dates than my original troupe had, often opening for the leading groups.

When I graduated from Anderson and got a job teaching junior high in the Anderson school system, I quit traveling and singing. Our pastor asked if I would take the choir at church. I didn't feel choral directing was my strength, but I agreed to do it anyway. I was not trained in formal church music, and my first love was singing in a group, but I knew that was a dead issue.

After a couple of years of teaching and directing the

choir, I started to notice what I considered a hole in Christian music. There seemed to be a gap in the area of personal expression; ideas needed to be communicated, but no songs existed to express them. Many of the songs of that time were good, and some were just okay. Others seemed as if they had some good elements, but I thought leaned toward the sentimental and needed more solid doctrine or theology. Some would have been better if their best elements had been blended with those from other tunes. A lot of the songs were about either being saved or going to heaven, which are, of course, things I believe in. But between those two realities we have a lot of living to do in this old world. It may seem presumptuous to think that despite the huge history of Christian music through the years there was still something only I could contribute, but most new ideas are brought into existence because of that felt need.

I kept in touch with people from the various singing groups, and one of my favorite singers was Jim Hill. He was from an Ohio quartet called the Golden Keys and had written a song called "What a Day That Will Be." He was a good singer, and when I thought of a song that needed to be written, I imagined him singing it. Many times writers write songs with certain vocalists in mind.

Finally, in 1960, I decided to try to write a song, a personal testimony about the fact that though I had never been to the Holy Land, spiritually I had been to Calvary. I saw it as a new birth song. The words and the music seemed to come together over a few hours, and I painstakingly picked them out and jotted them down. For all the insecurities I'd had as a pianist and a singer, when I finished my first composition, I felt a quiet confidence. With the Lord's help I had accomplished something—

something I likely would not have done if I had become an overnight success at nineteen or had hooked up quickly with a big touring gospel group. No, this had come about because of what I thought had been a colossal failure in my life. That setback had put me in a place where I had been forced to study literature and English and poetry, and where I had been exposed to a broader range of music.

Here's that first song, written at home when I was a young junior high school teacher:

I've Been to Calvary

I've never traveled far around the world,
I've never seen the many thrills and sights unfurled.
But I have taken the journey of journeys for me,
Up Calvary's mountain, there my Savior to see.

I walked the Calvary road where Jesus trod,
I saw Him hanging there, the Son of God!
With tear-stained eyes I knelt and prayed, "Jesus, hear
*   my plea";*
Oh, praise the Lord! I'm glad I've been to Calvary.

I've been to Calvary, I can say I've seen the Lord;
I've been to Calvary, through the witness of His Word;
Each day at Calvary, what a thrill of love divine,
Just to know that this Savior is mine! *

I finished and thought, *You know what? This is pretty good.* (In hindsight, it may not have been as good as I thought it was!) I drove to Ohio to teach it to my friend Jim Hill and the others in the Golden Keys. What a thrill to

*Words and Music by William J. Gaither. Copyright © 1960 BEN SPEER MUSIC, 920 Sutton Hill Road, Nashville, Tennessee.

hear them sing it! Nothing brings more joy to a writer than to hear his song sung well. Two weeks later they tried it in concert and Jim called me. "Bill," he said, "your song tore the place up."

Now I can now look back on what I thought was my failure at the back of that 4-H auditorium at the county fair in Ohio and see that it was, instead, a real beginning. If I hadn't "failed," I might still be beating around the country in the back of a bus, singing and playing my way from one town to the next without ever knowing the joy of adding one song to the kingdom of Christ and His church.

I wrote a few more songs for the Golden Keys to try out, and then got a call from Ben Speer of the great Speer Family, an established group. "The other night I heard the Keys sing 'I've Been to Calvary,' Bill. Do you have a publisher for that?"

My heart raced. "No."

"Would you be interested in our company's publishing that?"

Would I? Does Billy Graham have a quiet time?

Ben crafted a contract to cover that first song plus three or four others. Then the Speer Family recorded on the Skylight label "I've Been to Calvary," which was also recorded by many other artists. I knew then that things would start happening. I felt very good about knowing that others thought my songs were special, particularly someone established enough to have some credibility.

After that I wrote three songs: "In the Upper Room," "Lovest Thou Me More Than These?" and "Have You Had a Gethsemane?" which I felt were of better quality than the previous ones. At that point I started my own music company.

Just around the corner for me was yet another new beginning, but it had nothing to do with music.

CHAPTER FIVE

GROWING UP IN INDIANA

Have you prayed the night through?
Have you shed tears of agony when hope isn't
    in view?
Have you prayed, "If it be Thy will, may this
    cup pass from me,
But if it's Thy will, oh, Lord, I will bear it for
    *Thee"**

I was the oldest kid in the family and pretty much a driver. I had been raised with a solid Protestant work ethic that left me feeling uneasy and even a little guilty if I wasn't working—and working hard—most of the time. My growing up years had been a sort of a Huckleberry Finn experience without the big river. I spent my days on the farm milking three cows, getting them bedded down every night, being sure the gate was closed, baling hay, all that. We didn't take many vacations at all. Who would take care of the cows and the place?

Some of my clearest, though not fondest memories from that period are of working all day in the fields and suffering from hay fever. I would finally stagger into the bathtub and try to wash all that debris from my hair and eyes and ears, seeing it float on the water. Then I would make my way to a hot, upstairs bedroom where I tried to get enough sleep to be ready to get back at it the next day. Our parents and aunts and uncles spoke of the Great Depression and motivated us to be frugal and conservative and diligent. We grew up believing in hard work and security, family values, and patriotism.

It was during my childhood that I first started being concerned about the big Russian bear and the depressing cloud of communism that seemed to constantly hang over our heads. The United States was in Korea to halt communism. We would go to Vietnam to halt communism. For some reason, the communists threatened our security and our way of life. They wanted to dominate us, to take us over. Their leaders threatened to take over without ever firing a shot. Nikita Khrushchev said, "We will bury you!" It was a fearful, depressing time of bomb shelters and practice air raids. It wasn't until I visited the Soviet Union a couple of years ago that I realized we had been afraid of a paper tiger all those years. What a backward country technologically! It seemed nothing worked. From the dingy airport in Moscow where only every other ceiling light functioned, to the run-down look of the cities and the primitive telephone system, this appeared to be a superpower in name only.

As an adult, being a teacher, a songwriter, and a church musician kept me busy. I enjoyed teaching more than anyone might have predicted from my own academic background. Reading philosophy and broadening my worldview was new to me after having given up my dreams of a performing career. While I never considered myself an intellectual, I grew to really enjoy literature, language, and interacting with students and colleagues.

By the time I was twenty-six I had begun traveling and singing a little more because people who enjoyed my songs asked if we would come to their churches and sing them and talk about them. Between that and the church work, I was spending so much time on the road every day that I transferred to Alexandria High School at the beginning of the 1961–62 school year to be closer to home.

In January of 1962 I noticed a substitute French teacher down the hall and asked another teacher about her.

"That's Gloria Sickal from Battle Creek, Michigan," she said. "Her dad's a pastor up there, and she's a student at Anderson College."

"Is she married?"

"Nope."

"Why don't you introduce us?"

I wasn't really interested in marriage. I liked the freedom of my bachelor life, and I enjoyed dating around. And the substitute French teacher was pretty cute. We were introduced in the cafeteria and enjoyed lunch and a discussion of literature (she was also an English major) and politics. We didn't talk much music, and I didn't tell her I composed. She was not a musician and never claimed to be.

We seemed to hit it off right away and began seeing each other in the spring. After several dates I finally brought her to the house and played and sang a couple of songs for her. She noticed my name on the music.

"You write this stuff?"

"Yeah."

"It's pretty good."

I didn't know she would one day be the primary lyricist for my tunes, but I had always been attracted to poetic women, and she was certainly one. She also majored in sociology and had a minor in French. She was bright and "well-read," and she would graduate *cum laude;* "I was just thankful I graduated."

The more I got to know her, the more impressed I was. Despite my freedom and independence, I realized I was falling in love and that I would really be missing out on a wonderful opportunity if I didn't follow through on this one. Besides all her other attributes, she was truly and deeply spiritual. A lady like Gloria doesn't come around twice in a man's life. We were engaged in the summer and married December 22, 1962.

I was becoming more and more interested in getting good new music to other people. I asked my church if they would underwrite an album of choir music, mostly stuff I had written and arranged. They said no, so I sponsored "The South Meridian Sings" myself and saw it sell more than a thousand copies. So we recorded "The South Meridian Sings, Volume 2."

The assistant pastor, Paul Hart (who was also a musician), introduced me to a soloist from the Church of God named Doug Oldham. I loved his voice and the way he presented a song, but Doug was having a lot of trouble. Though his father was a well-known radio voice in the Church of God, and a musician in his own right, Doug's life was heading south very quickly. His family was in shambles and his wife had left him.

But he liked my song "Have You Had a Gethsemane?" because he was enduring a Gethsemane of his own. Because of the strife in his marriage and his spiritual failure, he saw the end of his dream. He had wanted to be a gospel singer all his life, but no one wanted to listen to a man who couldn't keep his family together. Doug had come to the end of his rope and turned back to God, committing himself anew to the Lord's will. He recorded my song, a very quiet, contemplative piece, and made it his own. He had come to grips with his failure and had been able to say, "Not my will, but Thine."

A couple of months later, he and his wife were reunited, and he was invited to sing at the annual convention of the Church of God. Usually the big, loud songs with the fancy endings turn on the crowd the most, but when Doug sang "Have You Had A Gethsemane?" a holy hush fell over the place. It's interesting that the Lord used this type of song to launch our publishing business.

Doug also sang "In the Upper Room with Jesus," and "Lovest Thou Me More Than These?" He interpreted them in such a way that we knew there was something special about them, and about Doug. His father—a preacher, a poet, and an ex-singer—had a lot of credibility with the church and with me. So when he said simply, "Bill, those are good songs; they're not run-of-the-mill," I took it as more than a typical compliment.

I frequently played the piano for Doug when he sang at his father's revival services, and sometimes we sang together. Doug's father often spoke about Doug's return to the Lord and how God had put his family back together. Dr. Oldham had just returned from the Holy Land and loved for Doug and me to sing "I've Been to Calvary." One night on the way to a service he was preaching in Huntington, Indiana, he hit me with a song idea.

"You ought to write a song called 'He Touched Me,' about how God changes lives."

"Interesting," I said.

That night we sang many of Doug's dad's favorites, but the following Sunday morning before church, I went to the piano and in a very short time wrote:

He Touched Me

Shackled by a heavy burden,
'Neath a load of guilt and shame,
Then the hand of Jesus touched me,
And now I am no longer the same.
Since I met this blessed Savior,
Since He cleansed and made me whole,
I will never cease to praise Him;
I'll shout it while eternity rolls:

He touched me, oh, He touched me.
And, oh, the joy that floods my soul.
Something happened and now I know,
He touched me and made me whole. *

The following Tuesday night, we were at another of Dr. Oldham's meetings. I handed Doug a copy of the music and suggested, "Sing this one tonight." We ran through it a few times, and he loved it. When he sang it for the people, something happened. Doug knew a good song when he heard it. Any time he felt the Spirit moving in the congregation, he returned to the lyric of the chorus and sang it through again. Four or five songs further into the program, he'd repeat the chorus again and again. It seemed to fit everywhere, and soon people were humming and singing it with him. By the end of that night they either loved the song or they didn't, but they sure knew it by heart! The demand for the printed music and the recording of that song kept us busy. It's funny: When the Lord is in something, you can't stop it.

Once I got the sheet music produced, Kathryn Kuhlman began using it on her radio broadcasts. Then the Speer Family started singing it. Ben Speer called one day and ordered three hundred copies of the sheet music. The next day he called and said, "We're out. Send us five hundred more." That's a scary and rewarding feeling—to know you've created something so meaningful to so many. You never know. I thought it was good, but I would never have predicted the kind of acceptance it has seen through the years. I was just a kid from a town in Indiana that's fifty miles out of your way no matter where you're going. I have never written for commercial success. I just wrote what was in my heart and in my gut. If it struck a chord, so be it. When God blesses a song, something happens over which I have no control.

As a young married man I was becoming so busy that I knew something had to give. The time finally came to quit directing music at church. Danny had gone to sing with the Golden Keys Quartet, so when people asked me to come and sing my songs at their churches, Gloria and Mary Ann and I went and did the best we could. I'm not begging for compliments when I say that we were less than adequate. I had proven to myself that I didn't have the talent to make a go of it with my voice, and Gloria never even wanted to be a singer. She had a pleasant enough blending voice, but she was not a professional and had a limited range.

When Gloria became pregnant with Suzanne, she dropped out and Danny came back. Now at least there was one powerful, professional voice among us. But when Mary Ann left to get married and start a family, we thought the group was dead. We tried a couple of other singers, including one young woman who was very good but for some reason simply didn't work with us stylistically.

I had agreed to bring a group to the Maiden Lane Church of God in Springfield, Ohio, one Sunday, but the Gaither Trio had unraveled. Being an old-fashioned trouper who never backs out of a commitment, I begged Gloria to step in with Danny and me as the third voice. "Honey, you've got to sing with us. I need you there."

"I can't sing," she said.

"I know you can't," I teased, "but you're pretty, you're a wonderful communicator, you've got a great spirit, you're my wife, and I need your help."

She reluctantly agreed, but we went that night feeling very inadequate. We called ourselves the Gaither Trio, but it was really Danny and the Schoolteachers. We opened with a Henry Slaughter tune called "I Never Loved Him Better Than Today" and followed with Doris Akers' "Sweet, Sweet Spirit." Then I asked Gloria to pray.

My wife, as many people know by now, has a way of articulating the passions of the heart. As she prayed, she touched the throne. She was not praying just for effect, but what an effect it had! I don't even remember what she said, but when we looked up at the end of that prayer, people all over the auditorium were weeping. God had anointed that place and that crowd and His three singers, even though two of us were truly weak.

Danny should not have been burdened with trying to carry us. It was nine years past the day when I had shelved my dream, and Gloria had never even pretended to be a vocalist. Yet in spite of our limitations, the Spirit of the Lord took control. It was a success in every way.

The pastor told us later that he had not seen that kind of audience response—people coming to Christ through our ministry—even in many evangelistic campaigns. We sold all the records and music we'd brought with us.

What was going on? I wasn't sure. On the way home in the car, I prayed silently, "Lord, are You trying to tell us something?" I felt so stupid. Gloria had clearly been the difference. Something in her spirit, her demeanor, her delivery had melted hearts. She had been under my roof all the time, but because she was clearly not a singer, I had not recognized the gift she had to offer.

She had enjoyed the evening because something had happened spiritually. Her original goal had been to study for the mission field, and now, virtually in her own back yard, she was ministering, reaching people for Christ.

Gloria was the extra ingredient that made the concert special, but when we recorded we used Betty Fair, a dear friend from Anderson. Gloria's role in the studio was to record some spoken word from her heart, something disc jockeys and listeners often referred to as her "readings." People began skipping over the songs to get to Gloria's readings. One pastor told me, "Bill, I usually encourage groups to do less talking and more singing. In your case, do less singing and more talking!" All because of Gloria.

She enjoyed being in on the concerts, despite her misgivings about her singing, but she did not want to perform in the studio in front of a bunch of pros. I didn't insist, but things wouldn't remain that way for long.

CHAPTER SIX

BACK HOME IN INDIANA

Jesus, Jesus, Jesus;
There's just something about that name!
Master, Savior, Jesus,
Like the fragrance after the rain;
Jesus, Jesus, Jesus,
Let all Heaven and earth proclaim;
Kings and kingdoms will all pass away,
But there's something about that name. *

T he producer of our first several records was a young man in Nashville named Bob MacKenzie. Bob is a human dynamo, opinionated, talented, and blunt. In fact, we're both such intense personalities that often we have confrontations, yet we each consider the other one of our dear, best friends.

Bob, or Mac as I most often call him, knew what he liked and didn't like, and he liked what happened in concerts with the early Gaither Trio. The first three records he produced with Betty Fair as the female remain three of the very best we've ever done, but Mac saw the magic of Gloria's participation in live performances. After hearing her sing with us and present the spoken part of *There's Something About That Name* at the First Baptist Church in Elkhart, Indiana, he thought it only right that she herself sing on the next album.

"You're singing in person," he said, "and when people buy the records, they think they're getting you. You've got to sing on the records."

"But I'm not a singer."

"I know you aren't," he said, "but I'll help you. Trust me. You're good enough for a concert; we'll make you good enough in the studio."

What Bob had heard in Elkhart was this, Gloria's thoughts during a musical interlude in *There's Something About That Name:*

Jesus.
The mere mention of His name can calm the storm, heal the broken, raise the dead. At the name of Jesus, I've seen sin-hardened men melted, derelicts transformed, the lights of hope put back into the eyes of a hopeless child. . . .
At the name of Jesus, hatred and bitterness turn to love and forgiveness, arguments cease.
I've heard a mother softly breathe His name at the bedside of a child delirious from fever, and I've watched that little body grow quiet and the fevered brow cool.
I've sat beside a dying saint, her body racked with pain, who in those final fleeting seconds summoned her last ounce of ebbing strength to whisper earth's sweetest name—Jesus, Jesus. . . .
Emperors have tried to destroy it; philosophies have tried to stamp it out. Tyrants have tried to wash it from

the face of the earth with the very blood of those who claim it. Yet still it stands.

And there shall be the final day when every voice that has ever uttered a sound—every voice of Adam's race—shall rise in one great, mighty chorus to proclaim the name of Jesus—for in that day "every knee shall bow and every tongue shall confess that Jesus Christ is Lord!"

Ah, so you see, it was not mere chance that caused the angel one night long ago to say to a virgin maiden, "His name shall be called JESUS."

Jesus, Jesus, Jesus . . . You know, there *is* something about that name.

For the album Bob MacKenzie had in mind, arranger Rick Powell went to London where the instrumental tracks were recorded. Then he brought them back and Danny and I and, yes, Gloria, went into the studio to add the vocals. By that time (1970), because of Gloria's involvement, the lyrics of my songs began to develop some real depth. She was gifted to articulate an idea in poetry that could touch people's hearts.

In those days, a Christian record selling more than ten thousand was a big success, and anything in the twenty-five to forty thousand range was off the charts. Our modest efforts had been in the six to eight thousand range. I can still remember when Wayne Buchanan, then marketing person at Benson, called to say, "Bill, you're not going to believe this, but 'Back Home in Indiana' is already at ten thousand sales." He was right; I didn't believe it.

Wayne called a few weeks later.

"You're not going to believe this," he began again. "'Back Home' is at twenty thousand."

That began a series of calls that I will never forget. Wayne enjoyed beginning each the same way: "You're not going to believe this, but . . . ," and I enjoyed hearing what came next. The calls informed me that the record had reached various sales plateaus, finally up to 300,000 units, the biggest album in Benson's history at that point. This was by a trio that included two people who didn't consider themselves singers, and one of these had never done a serious record before! All that showed me was the truth of Scripture that it's "not by might, nor by power, but by My Spirit, says the Lord."

People have speculated for years about what made that record work. I firmly believe God blessed Gloria's "Jesus" narration and also her reading of the second verse of "The King Is Coming," a song that had become a standard almost overnight. Frankly, none of us knew what to make of it. It was simply one of those anointed records.

The King Is Coming

The marketplace is empty,
No more traffic in the streets,
All the builders' tools are silent,
No more time to harvest wheat.

Busy housewives cease their labors,
In the courtroom no debate,
Work on earth is all suspended
As the King comes through the gate.

Happy faces line the hallways,
Those whose lives have been redeemed,
Broken homes that He has mended,
Those from prison He has freed;

Little children and the aged
Hand in hand stand all aglow,

Who were crippled, broken, ruined,
Clad in garments white as snow.

I can hear the chariots rumble,
I can see the marching throng,
The flurry of God's trumpets
Spells the end of sin and wrong;

Regal robes are now unfolding,
Heaven's grandstands all in place,
Heaven's choir is now assembled,
Start to sing Amazing Grace.

Oh, the King is coming! The King is coming!
I just heard the trumpet sounding
And now His face I see;
Oh, the King is coming! The King is coming!
Praise God, He's coming for me!*

Up to that point we had been singing in large churches, we then started appearing in high schools that would seat a thousand or so. When those venues began selling out in advance and we had to turn people away, we booked civic auditoriums that could accommodate two and three thousand people and finally moved our concerts to the twelve- to fifteen-thousand-seat arenas.

I have to tell you, it was pretty overwhelming. While we knew our own musical limitations, we loved the fact that people loved our work. God had clearly blessed us, and any artist enjoys knowing that people appreciate his work. One day, when I was sharing the excitement with arranger and friend Rick Powell, he asked how we were

*Words and Music by William J. and Gloria Gaither. Last stanza in part by Charles Millhuff. Music by William J. Gaither. Copyright © 1970 by William J. Gaither. International copyright secured. All rights reserved.

doing. We were young artists, and I told him I couldn't believe how many albums we were selling. I said, "Rick, the crowds at our concerts are unbelievable."

My dear friend motioned me close and whispered, "Bill, come here. Let me give you a bit of advice: Don't take it too seriously." I again recalled Kipling's thoughts on success and failure—take both impostors the same.

What great advice! I've often shared that with young artists. I had to ask myself if I *had* been taking it too seriously. You can get caught up in reading your own press releases, but I had been unaware I was doing that. I'm human and it was a lot of fun. Now I have years of perspective that allow me to see the wisdom of Rick's advice. Maybe without knowing it, he was saying, "This is temporary. This too shall pass. Truth is truth whether or not there is a big crowd." It helps to have friends help you keep things in perspective.

Bob MacKenzie was a wonderful friend in that regard because he was always quick to bring me down to earth when I seemed to be impressed with any success we might have. He would remind me of all the factors that went into making something work, like the sheer numbers of people involved in producing, arranging, packaging, marketing, and selling. Parts of success can be attributed to being in the right place at the right time, filling a vacuum. And if indeed a record was anointed of God to be a success in spite of all our weaknesses, who were we to take the credit or be impressed with ourselves?

In all fairness, it isn't surprising that I was a bit overwhelmed with it all. Having grown up hearing my dad and granddad talk about the Great Depression, I had become careful and frugal. I remember as a child asking my dad if we had enough of a reserve if something happened to him and he couldn't work anymore. I could hardly believe the good things that were happening after this album and was afraid of losing them. Where was the balance?

A major record can catapult an artist into a different sphere, and that happened to us with "Back Home in Indiana." The phone began to ring, and we were invited to perform in many places throughout the country. I knew instinctively that we either had to get control of that monster or it would control us. The temptation when your star begins to rise is to ride it for all it's worth. We could have easily booked ourselves into big arenas every night of the year and tried to capitalize, but what would that have done to us? Where would our family and our marriage be at the end of it? Where would our relationships with the Lord be?

When I thought it through, I concluded that God's will for my life could not be to run and jump every time the phone rang. We also felt it was not in our best interest or the interest of our family to leave our little town or the people who knew us well and still loved us. We had two young children by then, and we were committed to raising them in as normal a situation as our lives would allow.

Just eleven years before, I had hit a brick wall in my life and had to conclude, "Bill, you're not good enough to make your living with your fingertips and your vocal cords." Now the very dream I gave to God and put on the shelf, He gave back to me, in effect saying, "I think I can trust you with this now."

Was my voice any better? Did I play any better? Not that much. But I had been exposed to more, had matured emotionally and spiritually, and was doing what He had planned for me—composing—before I ever knew I had it in me. I don't want to be falsely modest. I feel as if the

Lord gifted me to put words and music together. Clearly, I was more ready to follow His leading at thirty than I had been at nineteen. If broad influence had come to me that early, there's no telling what might have become of me or of what He had entrusted to me.

There were other things I had never considered, such as the fact that some people enjoy shooting at those in the public eye. If you had asked me if I could handle that, I might have said yes. If you had asked me if I was prepared for it, I would have to say no. That was too bad. I didn't see it coming. And it almost destroyed me.

CHAPTER SEVEN

IN THE TUNNEL

Life is worth the living, just because He lives. *

Any writer will tell you that all he wants to do is write his song. But if the song catches on, it can complicate your life. A lot of our songs were being recorded by well-known celebrities. We were also getting into a lot of printed publications, including hymnals. It's a thrill to see your song in a hymnal.

Here we were, basically a couple of brothers from Indiana—one who could sing, one who couldn't, and a school teacher/poet who had been pressed into service. A nobody from nowhere, I had labored for years in the mu-

---

sic ministry, but seemingly overnight we went from ano-
nymity to high visibility.

For a few years I had enjoyed hearing local congregations sing our stuff, but I'll never forget the first time I
heard a foreign crowd sing "There's Something About
That Name." We were at the Shrine Auditorium in Los
Angeles. To hear six thousand people in what I thought
was a sophisticated, far-away city sing a song by a farm kid
from Indiana, well, I was taken aback. I just wept. It's one
thing to write a song, and it's another to get a great artist to
record it and to see it well arranged and accompanied by a
great orchestra. That's all exciting. But, boy, when it gets
into the hands of regular folks and they treat it as they treat
their favorite old hymns, that is very special.

The country had just emerged from a decade of tremendous achievement and yet deep pain. Astronauts had
walked on the moon, but leaders had been struck down
too. John F. Kennedy, Robert F. Kennedy, and Martin
Luther King, Jr., had been assassinated. There had been
riots and looting, even death on college campuses. The
"God Is Dead" debate had raged during the 1960s too.
The 1968 Democratic National Convention in Chicago
had become an ugly spectacle. All that negativity gnawed
at the back of my mind, having been raised under the
threat of communism and with memories of the Depression recounted nearly every day. Somehow, the decade we
had come out of and the warnings I had grown up with
didn't mesh with all the good things that were happening
in our ministry.

I didn't know I was vulnerable to attack. But when
something in the core of your being questions your wor-
thiness for such honor and responsibility, you're only a
step away from self-doubt. And when someone puts the

question to you, face to face, it can stagger you—which was what happened to me.

A close acquaintance (not a Christian) was, I believe, jealous of what the Lord was doing. He questioned my motives, my commitment. That cut me to the heart. I had been careful. I had scrambled to keep my priorities straight. We were expecting our third child and were planning ways to keep control of the crazy schedule that otherwise threatened to overtake our lives. But why were we in this business? Did we just want to become rich and famous?

I should have known that God knew my heart, but a musician frequently wears his heart on his sleeve, and I was much more fragile than I knew. I had struggled to corral my priorities. We had taken some good advice from our friend Bob Reardon, about setting our financial priorities and establishing a good giving pattern. He knew we could get pulled in every direction. That was a step in the right direction for us. It was part of our effort to remain on an even keel. But I had not foreseen every attack.

The rumblings about our motives continued. I didn't want to believe it and I didn't believe it, but still it worked on me. Perhaps I was obsessed about motives because of my humble origins and my discomfort with all of a sudden being a person of some means. In hindsight, it's easy to say I should have let such things roll off my back and go about my business. But I was sensitive to reproof, and it made little difference whether that reproof or the person offering it had any validity.

I heard this acquaintance was saying I was in the business only for financial reasons. Nothing could have been further from the truth. Any real artist, Christian or not, would quickly tell you that he would create his art whether he ever made a dime from it or not. In my heart, I knew that works of art that passed the test of time have always been produced from the gut, not for commercial gain. Sure, there are songs and movies and stories that make a brief flash because they play on some emotion or have some unusual twist that captures the imagination for a time. And their originators collect a quick windfall. But the classics, those works that last for decades, are— without exception—creations from where the originator lives and breathes. The great Hank Williams classic, "I'm So Lonesome I Could Cry," was written without a dollar in mind. That was clearly created by a man with a lump in his throat and a tear on his cheek.

We write our songs from our hearts. I had given myself to the Lord and His service when I felt my music career was over at age nineteen. Gloria and I knew our motives. But by the time the rumors of criticism became fact, I had been weakened by stress and a bout with mononucleosis, and I was as susceptible to defeat as a young man can be. Then at a huge gathering my accuser cornered me and leveled the charges personally. There would be no more wondering, no more private debates with myself, trying to bolster my psyche against unconfirmed reports that someone was questioning me.

"You're a phony," he said, "and you know it."

"That's not true," was all I could manage.

"If you didn't make a living doing what you do, you wouldn't believe it."

I was speechless. This man truly believed what he was saying. He may have been motivated by jealousy, envy, or insecurity, but if his motive was to stop me in my tracks and make my life miserable, if he sought some perverse joy from my torment, he succeeded. Hardly realizing what was happening, my illness and that devastating charge sent me into a black hole. Though our lives continued in their busy way and we still traveled and sang and played and performed and ministered, I was suddenly unable to do the one thing I had been called to do: compose music.

Our ministry had gone from nothing to everything, and my pace had accelerated to where I was running every minute, but suddenly my legs had been yanked out from under me. I had no power, no footing. We were still praised by colleagues, filling auditoriums, seeing people moved by our songs and our concerts. But privately my confidence was shaken. What would the future hold if I couldn't produce any new music?

Gloria stood strong. She was doing fine. She still came up with ideas and snippets and verses and poems, all that creative stuff that used to get me started on a tune. But I was gridlocked. Almost immediately I assumed the worst. I quickly decided that the ride would soon be over. It had been nice while it lasted, I told myself, but nothing that good and fun and exciting lasts forever. I thanked God that we had been used for that brief season of years, but I heard nothing from Him. It was as if the door of heaven had slammed shut.

I was depressed. There's no other explanation for it. Some days I was so weak all I could do was sit or lie on my back and let the tears roll. Gloria tried to cheer me, to encourage me, but nothing is lower than an emotional low after the kind of joy we had experienced. I felt as if I had reversed direction in an instant and had gone from being the best thing since ice cream to something that had been run over by a Mack truck. Nothing can hurt a poet and a creator more than an attack on his motives.

I saw no sliver of light in my long, dark tunnel. Not even the news of the continuing success of the music and the trio lifted my spirits. I mustered the energy and the courage to fulfill our commitments, but that made me feel more of a phony than ever. I was not as high and as happy as I appeared, and I began to doubt myself. Doug Oldham's father, Doug himself, Bob MacKenzie, and Bob Benson would tell me they believed in me, to pull out of this, to remember who I was and Whose I was. *Phony, phony, phony,* rattled in my brain.

Month after month dragged by as my gift, my talent, was paralyzed. I've never been one to quickly attribute every malady that comes along to a satanic attack, but I do believe a spirit of evil has been let loose in this world, and we're kidding ourselves if we don't think we're engaged in spiritual warfare. Depression is so dark and ugly that I believe Satan usually plays a major part in it.

I had no peace. No one can create any kind of art if it's not something he or she really loves to do. But now every time I forced myself to sit at the piano, blank sheet on the rack and pencil in hand, looming in my brain was that seed of doubt that had been planted, had taken hold, had been watered, and was now beginning to flourish.

Why are you writing this?

"Because it's something I believe in."

Are you sure?

"I thought I was."

Fake. Phony. Selfish. Bad motives.

And I was finished for another day.

Meanwhile, new life was growing again inside Gloria. She and my closest friends were worried about me, and rightfully so. I knew better than to let this get me down, but I had been wounded, cut deeply by criticism I wanted to believe was wrong and ill motivated. But I couldn't shake it. I didn't want to hurt anybody. Part of my nature longed for everyone to like me, for all to know that I had pure motives. If one person believed I was phony, what did others think?

The dream was waning. Was it over? Was this then the extent of the body of work Bill Gaither and the Trio would contribute to the cause of the kingdom? I was frantic, desperate to exercise my gift again. We were scheduled to cut another album not long after our baby was due. Could I pull myself together and try to make something happen?

I knew I could do nothing without the Lord, but He still seemed silent to me. I pleaded for His help and decided that I would try to proceed regardless of how I felt. That upbringing of mine was a double-edged sword because, whatever negative aspects there were to it, there was also that sense of duty, of responsibility, of doing things because they had to be done.

The birth of our only son, Benjy, helped bring me out of my depression. It was so wonderful to see that new little life come into the world, and I knew I had to be a fully-functioning father for him and his two big sisters. Gloria and I talked of how sweet it was to hold a new baby and feel that pride and joy that comes from God. I still feared raising our children in such uncertainty, of ups and downs, of unfair attacks. Could I face the future? Was life worth living?

Gloria and I were thrilled with Benjy, of course, and were inspired to put a few thoughts on paper, which became the basis for a new song. All through the process I kept telling myself—and she continually encouraged me—that this, this task, is what we are all about. I knew I would believe what she and I had written and that we would write it and bank on it spiritually whether or not it ever produced a dime of income.

When we put the finishing touches on the piece, I knew we had created something of value, again without caring about its commercial potential. It portrayed truth and beauty and the deepest thoughts of our hearts. Maybe someone with a selfish, commercial motive could express something like that, but I doubt it. God had reentered my life through the beauty of the birth of our son, through the encouragement and prayers and concerns of my wife and closest friends, and through a work ethic that propelled me to the piano to finish a message He had given me.

Because He Lives

God sent His Son, they called Him Jesus;
He came to love, heal, and forgive;
He lived and died to buy my pardon,
An empty grave is there to prove my Savior lives.

How sweet to hold our newborn baby,
And feel the pride and joy he gives;
But greater still the calm assurance,
This child can face uncertain days because He lives.

And then one day I'll cross that river;
I'll fight life's final war with pain;
And then as death gives way to victory,
I'll see the lights of glory and I'll know He reigns.

Because He lives I can face tomorrow;
Because He lives all fear is gone;

Because I know He holds the future,
*And life is worth the living just because He lives!**

That was not the only good song to come out of that horrible experience. I had finally answered the motive question to my own satisfaction and said, "No! I'm not doing this for the wrong reasons; I'm doing this because it is the stuff I've thought through and lived and believed in." Once again I would have to look back and ask myself if that bout with severe depression was the setback I thought it was. Did I lose or did I win? I was definitely rained out for a while.

As with most adverse situations, I grew in tremendous ways that would have been lost to me if I had just merrily sailed on to greater heights. What had happened to me in the deepest, darkest moments of my waning faith was a return to the simplicity of the message of God's love for me. When all else was gone, when my first love had turned to dust, I clung by my fingernails to the cross of Calvary. Jesus and what He had done for me became the only things that really mattered to me.

There was something poignant about a Midwestern boy-turned-man coming full circle to the basic, unadorned simplicity of his faith. With deep emotion I felt led to write an exuberant song.

My Faith Still Holds

I tried to find life's mysteries,
Just by the reason of my mind to see,
But void remained 'tween me and where I longed to be,
'Til childlike faith there built a bridge for me.

*Words by William J. and Gloria Gaither. Music by William J. Gaither. Copyright © 1971 by William J. Gaither. International copyright secured. All rights reserved.

I thought I had to see and feel,
To prove that what I loved was really real,
But passion turned to ashes, things I held to dust,
I found reality in simple trust.

And oh what joy to walk this way!
I follow nail-pierced footprints all the way,
And though the end of where I'm bound I may not see,
I choose to place my trust in Calvary.

Now years have passed since in my youth
I weathered storms of doubt in search of truth.
Sweet Jesus calmed the tempest of my soul's unrest,
Praise God! The Calvary Road has stood the test.

My faith still holds on to the Christ of Calvary,
Oh, blessed Rock of Ages cleft for me.
I gladly place my trust in things I cannot see,
My faith still holds on to the Christ of Calvary. *

CHAPTER EIGHT

SOMETHING BEAUTIFUL

*All I had to offer Him was brokenness and strife . . . ***

"*B*ecause He Lives" didn't

take off as explosively as "He Touched Me" or "The King
Is Coming," but it was one of those theological statements
people knew was real because it had come out of the
nitty-gritty of living.

One Monday morning, after a wonderful weekend of
singing and seeing people respond to "Because He Lives,"
Gloria and I were marveling over God's goodness. We
looked at our three precious children and thought of the
experience of sharing that song with appreciative people

*From "Something Beautiful" by William J. and Gloria Gaither. Copy-
right © 1971 by William J. Gaither. International copyright secured. All
rights reserved.

and how that had warmed our hearts. "You know what?" I said, "Despite all this stuff we've been going through, God has still done something beautiful in our lives."

It doesn't take much to get Gloria started thinking and writing. Not long after that she came to me with a poem that would become the lyric for "Something Beautiful," a hauntingly pretty tune, I think, that came to me gradually as I studied her work. We began singing it at every concert.

Something Beautiful

If there ever were dreams that were lofty and noble,
They were my dreams at the start.
And the hopes for life's best were the hopes that I
harbored
Down deep in my heart.

But my dreams turned to ashes, my castles all crumbled,
My fortune turned to loss,
So I wrapped it all in the rags of my life,
And laid it at the cross!

Something beautiful, something good;
All my confusion, He understood.
All I had to offer Him was brokenness and strife,
But He made something beautiful of my life. *

At a concert in New Jersey soon after, the crowd was a beautiful racial and ethnic mix, and the emotion ran high. We sensed from the beginning that the people were with us. They were excited, upbeat, and enthusiastic. It seemed we could do no wrong. The happy, energized tunes were applauded and cheered, people sang along, and we were having a good time. The quieter, more worshipful songs hushed the crowd, and it was like having church with them.

We had saved "Because He Lives" and "The King Is Coming" for the finale, but I was frustrated. By the end we sensed the cheering and adulation was directed more toward us than toward God.

We're as human as anyone, so we enjoy a certain amount of attention and encouragement. For the Christian performer, it's a fine line to walk. But we strive to bring glory to God, and frankly that kind of a reaction made me a little uncomfortable. I was embarrassed as we left the stage. The emcee called us back out for another bow, and the easy thing would have been to move into another refrain of either of the last two songs. But I felt led to redirect that attention to where it belonged. It hadn't been that long since I had been a wounded, confused, defeated warrior, off the front lines, unable to write because of an attack on my motives. I certainly wasn't in a frame of mind to ignore all that and pretend that such praise from a generous audience was due me or the Trio.

As we came back on stage to more cheering and whistling, I slid onto the piano bench, thanked the crowd, and motioned to them to sit and quiet themselves, then began softly playing, "Oh, How I Love Jesus." Danny and Gloria joined in, and we sang a simple, soft harmony of that classic.

There is a name I love to hear,
I love to sing its worth.
It rings like music in my ears,
The sweetest name on earth.

Oh, how I love Jesus.
Oh, how I love Jesus.
Oh, how I love Jesus,
Because He first loved me.

Almost immediately I sensed the adoration of the crowd had been directed upward. They had not been ill motivated or inappropriate. They had loved and cherished and honored Jesus all night. They simply needed a little traffic direction to get their eyes off the messengers and onto the reason for the message.

Later I told Gloria, "Honey, we need a song of our own that sums up the evening and ends the concert on a note of praise and worship." That was all she needed to hear. Fresh from that experience, she wrote the perfect lyric to a song that would close our programs.

Let's Just Praise the Lord

We thank you for your kindness,
We thank you for your love,
We've been in heavenly places,
Felt blessings from above;
We've been sharing all the good things
The family can afford,
Let's just turn our praise toward heaven
And praise the Lord!

Just the precious name of Jesus
Is worthy of our praise,
Let us bow our knee before Him,
Our hands to heaven raise;
When He comes in clouds of glory,
With Him to ever reign,
Let's lift our happy voices
And praise the Lord.

Let's just praise the Lord! Praise the Lord!
Let's just lift our hands to heaven, and praise the Lord!
Let's just praise the Lord! Praise the Lord!
Let's just lift our hands toward heaven and praise the
    *Lord!**

Bob MacKenzie invited Ronn Huff, a great arranger and producer, to a few of our concerts. Mac thought Ronn would be impressed by the worship experience that resulted. I told jokes, exaggerated my occasional stammer, and tried to have fun. People seemed to enjoy it, and they stayed with us when we waxed serious, enjoyed the thrill of the big, rousing songs, and were reverent during the quiet ones. Just when we'd reached the heights with "The King Is Coming" and "Because He Lives," we'd come back with "Let's Just Praise the Lord." We had the feeling that people left believing they'd had an experience with the Lord, but we weren't prepared for Ronn Huff's enthusiasm.

Here was a giant in the Christian music industry, a man many considered a genius, who believed that our type of concert could be made into a musical that churches could perform. We were skeptical, but honored and intrigued. We listened. He selected some songs from our concerts, including "Something Beautiful," "Because He Lives," "Get All Excited," "There's Something About That Name," "The King Is Coming," "The Longer I Serve Him," "Let's Just Praise the Lord," and several others.

Ronn arranged and rewrote and worked with us on order and spoken parts, then put several singers together with us so we could do a demo tape that would show how churches might stage the musical he called "Alleluia! A Praise Gathering for Believers."

The demo tape was fun and exciting because of all the talent that was pulled together for it, but none of us realized what we were involved in. What had been intended as a demo to help choirs catch the vision served that purpose, also sold as an album on its own.

As more and more choirs put on the musical, more and more people wanted a permanent record of the songs. We received mail from all over the country about city-wide cooperatives, various churches telling us they had worked with other denominations for the first time—charismatics uniting with evangelicals, Baptists with mainliners, and so forth. Meanwhile, the record kept selling. The unexpected bonus was a gold record—the Lord has an interesting sense of humor.

If we thought we'd been something of a phenomenon before, this was a whole new chapter in our existence. We knew better than to think we were something special. After my year of depression, I knew what and who I was. When I read the lyrics of my own songs, I knew that the only One worthy of any praise and credit was the Lord Himself. More than ever it was crucial that we keep our priorities straight, that we have a place to give our resources, that we focus on our roots and our home, our town and our state.

If God had seen fit to bless us with widespread acceptance, based on art that had come from within, we would have to be wise and wary. Visibility and the attendant schedule of such a life had the potential to take our eyes off our values, off our God, and even off our family. We didn't want to let that happen.

I began dreaming of being efficient and practical with our opportunities so that we could be in our home church on Sundays, have our kids travel with us when possible, and not get so caught up in material things that we were tempted to leave our geographical anchor. One of my earliest songs had been used on the "Alleluia" album, and its sentiments came to mind as I considered what was happening to the Bill Gaither Trio. I had written the song as a relatively young man six or so years before, but it was the type of tune sung by a senior citizen in the musical. Beyond doubt I wanted to be able to look back one day and still be able to sing that simple lyric of devotion. It wouldn't be easy, but if we could manage to corral our priorities, it would become the hallmark of our ministry and set the tone for what we hoped to accomplish with our lives. We would not be without hurdles and challenges, some I never could have anticipated, but my goal was to keep the foundation solid and focused.

The Longer I Serve Him

Since I started for the kingdom,
Since my life He controls,
Since I gave my heart to Jesus,
The longer I serve Him, the sweeter He grows.

Every need He is supplying,
Plenteous grace He bestows;
Every day my way gets brighter—
The longer I serve Him, the sweeter He grows.

The longer I serve Him, the sweeter He grows;
The more that I love Him, more love He bestows.

Each day is like heaven, my heart overflows—
The longer I serve Him, the sweeter He grows. *

CHAPTER NINE

A STUDENT OF LIFE

Being lied about, don't deal in lies,
Or being hated don't give way to hating.
—Rudyard Kipling

*I*t's only as I look back on my life and on the amazing development of our music company and performing groups that I get a handle on an honest, realistic self-analysis. The only trouble is, I didn't set out to be autobiographical here, so forgive me if I try to make a few points by citing some of what I've learned along the way. If you were hoping for a definitive assessment of my life, trust me, you would have been bored anyway. I may be a sort of jack of all trades within my profession, but I don't see myself as a terribly complex guy. I have an artist's temperament—with all the good and bad that goes with that—but what you see is pretty much what you get.

I see myself as a teacher, using my other skills and gifts to get that done. A prerequisite to teaching is learning, so I've needed to become a student of life. If there's one thing I've learned over the years, it's the importance and the beauty of the body of Christ. Twila Paris wrote a wonderful song called "How Beautiful Is the Body." I won't attempt to say better than she has that, in essence, we Christians are all part of this body and we dare not say we don't need each other. Much as the artist in me wishes he could do it all himself—writing, singing, playing, performing, producing, arranging, directing, publishing—I can't. I need people. The same is true in the church. We are not complete without each other, and that's why my philosophy has always been—or, I should say, has grown to become—one of looking for long-term results in people. If you expect too much too soon from a frail human, you'll find to your disappointment that he is as weak and mortal as you are.

I have striven over the years to eliminate class-consciousness from my thinking. What ugly, ungodly things are prejudice, bigotry, racism, provincialism, chauvinism. I have learned much from people with whom I supposedly should have little in common. I'm a generalist at heart and have an interest in many things. I love politics. I love sports, particularly professional basketball. And, of course, I love music. I can get interested in just about anything because of my student mindset. And I learn real-life lessons from many unrelated events in my life. I don't know what went into my genes to make me that way, but curiosity defines me.

On Thanksgiving Eve a few years ago, we noticed water gurgling in the pipes of our home. A local plumber, Mr. Maynard (who worked with his son and grandson), told me that his roto-rooter extended so far into the pipes without finding the blockage that he would have to go out into the property to locate it. Our system ran more than four hundred feet to where it attached to the city sewer system, and his rooter was only a hundred feet, so he asked if I knew where the drainage tile was buried in the ditch. I thought I did. I drove a stake into the ground and the plumber followed with a long, thin rod, trying to hit the tile. He found nothing.

The only option then was to bring in a back hoe and dig up the yard, looking for the drainage tile. Gloria and I gulped, but we had no choice. Mr. Maynard soon found the source of the trouble, a blockage in the system, but by now it was late Wednesday night and the next day was Thanksgiving. They would be back Friday. Since the music company was closed for the holidays, I was free to continue watching the plumbers do their work all day Friday. Nobody could understand what kept my interest, but as I say, I'm a student of life and fascinated by many disciplines.

With the rooter they determined where the blockage was and also that I had come within inches of the drainage tile with my stake. I had helped lay that tile twenty-five years before, and I had also mowed above it for years and knew where the yard dipped (and where the grass was greener).

The blockage was solid, so the men kept at it. There was still a lot of sludge that they couldn't get moving, so they called the city water department for a pressure hose. When they forced water into the drainage tile, the thing finally blew open like Old Faithful and shot fifty feet into the air. The four of us ran to get out from under the spray, laughing and clapping as if we'd struck oil—only it wasn't oil!

Gloria and the kids wondered what in the world I had been doing out there all day, watching the Maynards snaking through our sewer line. In truth, there was little that could have torn me away. Here were three generations of plumbers, treating each other with deference and respect, doing a wonderful service for us and our community, and doing it with obvious joy. I had learned a lot just by watching.

We kidded each other the whole time because of exactly what we were playing in, and I told them, "I do this every day of my life. This is the kind of stuff that's in people's lives, clogging the flow." Some way or another there comes a time when you have to do major surgery, like they did on my yard. But come spring we'd resow the grass and a fresh patch of green would heal the wound.

Well, I knew there was a sermon, or at least a lesson, in there somewhere. The more I thought about that little analogy, the more obvious it became that the clogged sewer was very much like a life that had shut down. It was plugged in only one place, but that stopped the whole mechanism, and nothing would flow again until the blockage was removed. The problem had festered under the surface where it went undetected until it affected the system; it had not built up overnight. Blockages in sewers, just like those that affect our lives, start small and continue to build, sometimes for years.

I wish sewers and life would offer earlier warning signs. Had I been alerted to the problem in my drainage tile, I would have sent something through the pipes to remedy it before it got out of hand. Sometimes my whole life seems to consist of watching for those little warning signs so I can deal with problems as early as possible. The sooner we confront issues head on, the sooner we know whether they constitute wins, losses, or rain-outs—which impostor was this, failure or success?

Following the wide acceptance of "Alleluia! A Praise Gathering For Believers," I discovered what life in the fishbowl is really like. It isn't that we became celebrities, but with more visibility we did lose a measure of our privacy. The more visible you are, the more of a target you become for criticism and unsolicited advice. I want to always be able to say I am open to either, but there's a way to evaluate someone else's work and a way not to. When you question someone's motives, the victim becomes defensive. And when personal lives are brought into question, someone has overstepped the bounds of propriety.

For instance, I can't tell you the number of wild rumors that have surfaced about Gloria and me and our family over the years. After you get into the public eye, it's amazing the outrageous rumors that get started about you and your ministry. When you first hear these kinds of things you wonder if people are serious! Many times the rumors are very hurtful. You finally have to harden yourself to them or they will destroy you.

One doesn't want to become defensive and speak about rumors in public, yet anyone in the public eye will be shot at. The trick is to take it graciously and treat the attackers in a Christlike way.

In fact, I can remember when my brother, Danny, left the group in the mid-1970s. There was a lot of misunderstanding about the situation, and we all felt great pain over the decision. A lot of details were too personal to share then, and they still are. The feelings run too deep. Living in a small town, though, it was hard to keep private pain to ourselves. Everybody around us knew us well, and naturally many took sides. At that point we were ready to hang it up and quit singing. Once again Bob MacKenzie offered his help and his friendship.

"Bill," he said, "do you really want to totally give up your public platform at this age? You don't have to. I'll help you put something else together."

In many ways what grew from that was one of the best things that ever happened to the Gaither singers. We started an annual "Praise Gathering for Believers" in Indianapolis that kicked off our continuing use of guest artists as part of our "Gaither and Friends" family. We put together the New Gaither Vocal Band with Gary McSpadden, Steve Green, and others, added Gary to the trio, and began introducing new talent at all our concerts—people like Don Francisco, Sandi Patti, Carman, and more. Years later, when Gary moved on, we persuaded Larnelle Harris and Michael English to join us for a while. The names and the chemistry kept changing, but the ministry continued.

Still, I could never look back on that time of estrangement from my brother as a win just because our performing groups expanded. Make no mistake, musically we were strong with Danny's voice and always would have been. But my most significant memory of that time is that Danny and I had a severed relationship and broken hearts.

Gloria and I took the position that we would always be there for Danny. Sadly, when we did come back together as loving brothers, Danny had throat problems and hasn't been able to sing much since. The loss of his voice was a very big price to pay, but at least thank God for the wonderful relationship we have now. We are closer than ever.

I've always said it's important for a Christian, just like a good quarterback, to stay in the pocket and not panic.

That's a tough lesson, but once you learn it, it offers great rewards. It's interesting that I was not vulnerable to depression during the bad times with Danny, probably because I had developed some spiritual muscle or perhaps some resistance during my first bout. I think God uses each struggle to prepare us for a bigger battle down the road. Every time we fight one, we know there is another around the next bend.

Our ministry had exploded, and only because we were dedicated to some unshakable principles were we able to keep up with it. We'll never regret the decision to attend our own home church almost every Sunday morning during those incredibly hectic years. Even though the crowds were unbelievable, we had learned long before to realize that this was God's anointing and blessing. That kept us from taking any undue credit for the influence of the ministry.

Our little sheet music business had really blossomed, and soon the Gaither Music Company began to expand. We got mail from all over the country thanking us for what our music was doing in the lives of churches, and that gave us the idea that we should continue to dream of ways to expand and multiply our outreach. We might minister before thousands, but that was nothing like the influence our records could have on hundreds of thousands, or even millions, if we packaged it correctly.

We tried to think of ways to do things better, to get our message into the world in the broadest ways possible. The "Alleluia" record and musical was one way. When Bob MacKenzie left the Benson Company in 1975, he and I formed Paragon and developed a new hymnal that came from the collective minds of Gloria, Ronn Huff, Fred Bock, Mac, me, and many others. It was an answer to the question, "Can we do something in a hymnal that's never been done?"

We were flush from the excitement of coming out of the depression days to the "Because He Lives" time of victory, and we knew that a hymnal with lots of our music in it would allow churches to replicate what we would otherwise have to bring to them live or on a record. We called the hymnal *Hymns for the Family of God,* and it became the first of its kind to contain readings strewn throughout the book. It also contained several other innovations, some good, some trendy.

The success of that hymnal was another high-water mark on our journey, but we were learning never to rest too comfortably. There is no time to relax and coast spiritually. If it's true that success and failure are both impostors and that only the long perspective of time helps determine whether we have won or lost, it's also true that we tend to learn more and become more mature through the difficult times.

I don't want to give the impression that this life of hard lessons was mostly depressing. It wasn't, and it still isn't. Frequently, the Lord put in our path some joy- or humor-filled moment that served as sugar to help the medicine go down, and we learned valuable lessons without going through the usual pain—like the Mr. Indiana story coming up.

CHAPTER TEN

I AM LOVED

I could hardly comprehend His offer:
*I'd give all I had—He'd give the rest!**

W hen Benjy was three or four years old and very impressionable, he was a hero worshiper and I was his hero. With a mom and two older sisters, naturally he identified more with me. In his eyes, I could do no wrong.

Well, one Sunday Mr. Indiana came to our church. As I recall his story, he had overcome some illness or physical handicap as a child and had grown up to become a body builder, a weight lifter, and a tremendous specimen of a man. He was also a wonderfully outspoken Christian.

*From "I Am Loved" by William J. and Gloria Gaither. Copyright ©
1978 by William J. Gaither. International copyright secured. All rights reserved.

During the evening service, our whole family sat there with our eyes bugging out as Mr. Indiana ran through his feats of strength. At one point he put a piece of cloth in his mouth to protect his teeth, then bit down on a long metal rod and bent it in two with his massive arms. It was incredible, and Benjy couldn't keep his eyes off the man. Frankly, neither could Gloria, Suzanne, or Amy.

That night at home and the next morning at breakfast, all I heard from the whole family was Mr. Indiana, Mr. Indiana, Mr. Indiana. I could understand Benjy's fascination, but Gloria's? I had heard enough. I said, "Aw, he's not so tough. I could beat him up." (Of course, I had checked to be sure he had already left town.)

Gloria and the girls laughed. Benjy didn't. "What, Dad? What?".

"I said I could beat up Mr. Indiana."

"Honest?"

"Yeah. I could take him."

The Gaither women howled, and that clearly bothered Benjy.

That evening when the kids gathered on our bed to watch a little television with us, I got an idea. I slipped out and stripped down to my boxer shorts, got a plastic drinking straw from the kitchen, and burst into the bedroom, posing like Mr. Indiana, straw in my teeth. One hundred and eighty pounds of unleashed fury, I strained and strained and turned red working on that straw until finally I bent it in two.

"That proves it!" I shouted, fists aloft. "I'm just as tough as Mr. Indiana!"

Gloria and the girls fell off the bed laughing. Benjy was clearly offended for me. He looked at them and looked at me, back at them and back at me, and tears formed. "Well, maybe that was just a straw," he said, "but it was a strong straw!"

I realized quickly how important I was to Benjy and how early he had begun learning what masculinity was. He really wanted to believe that his average-sized dad, a white-collar worker, was tough and strong. To Benjy I *was* Mr. Indiana. It was very important to him to have a role model of masculinity. Over the years, with the exception of that silly charade, I've tried to model true masculinity for my son by balancing the Mary and Martha elements in my life.

What became an even bigger challenge to me over the years was the balancing of those Mary and Martha elements in my business life. The more complex our business became, the tougher was the challenge. Gloria was acutely aware of my struggle from the beginning. Her father had pastored in Michigan until he had a heart attack, then he and Gloria's mother moved near us and helped with our fledgling business. We had started in our family room, filling sheet music orders for people interested in our stuff. But as the demand grew, so did our need for space and help, and Mom and Dad Sickal were a big help with the business and with the kids.

Gloria had always leaned toward the eternal values side of life, so creating special moments and making memories was a big thing with her. The artistic side of me appreciated that, too, but the business and our schedule began to dominate my life. Naturally, that led to some tension. So did the fact that we were now truly working together. When you write songs together, you make value judgments about each other's work. If she was shy about that in the beginning, she quickly learned not to be, because I sure wasn't. I was blunt and honest—for the sake of the current creation, of course—and she learned to speak her mind and defend herself. When your mate criticizes or questions your work, it can be pretty threatening. Who was she to have an opinion on my music? Who was I to have an opinion about her lyrics?

Even with those I love the most, I sometimes keep things inside and can carry a grudge. There's not a good reason for it. It's not admirable, and I'm certainly not proud of it. I've had to pray for grace and ask God to help me grow up and grow out of it. I'm thankful there's grace for that, just as there is for any sin.

Often, men internalize and wonder why women don't understand. Meanwhile, women wonder why men can't see what's really important. While Gloria and I have had to work to overcome such differences, the blending of our personalities has also helped us in our mission. It would be easy to pretend that we always see eye to eye, and some may feel more comfortable believing that about us. But there is value in being open, honest, and vulnerable. I don't know of any long-term relationship that hasn't had its share of struggles. God has taken our extremes and helped us do what we do together, but it has not been without disagreement.

Because we are both artists and poets, our highs are very high and our lows can be very low. In fairness to Gloria, I have to say her lows are not as low as mine. She can take the lows in stride much more easily. Being a wordsmith, a poet, an extraordinary communicator, singing is merely an avocation. She wants to do her best all the time, but like everyone else in the world, she has her own set of limitations. Singing is not her strongest point.

God has a weird sense of humor in giving a person just one gift and forcing him to work with others to get a job done. Of course, He did that on purpose, because if Gloria was a great singer, besides all of her other qualities, she might be impossible to live with. In truth, she's not as bad a singer as she thinks she is (nor as bad as my impatience with her sometimes must communicate). We both give her less credit than she deserves. Look at Bob Dylan. Now there's a guy who's not a great singer, but that hasn't hurt his career and influence.

Every time I go into the studio with Gloria, I resolve to remember that she never wanted to be nor claimed to be a singer. It is not her singing that has brought her to the place of ministry in which she finds herself. It's her ability to communicate and her wonderful, warm heart, her ability to put words together. She does this for me because I asked her to and I should be patient and appreciate her. Then in the heat of the battle, I forget.

Anybody who knows music knows that the studio is one place where the real test of relationships comes. We have to keep going back to repair Gloria's part and my part, and after every album we would joke that our marriage has survived yet another record.

Things grow tense because of my impatience and perfectionism. Rather than reminding myself that Gloria is doing her best, I can't understand why she can't hear when she is off. I walk her through the notes, sing them for her, point them out on the charts. When she gets frustrated, she reminds me that the only reason she is submitting to this is because she married me. That pressure builds throughout a recording session, and then we eat together and sometimes work until late into the night. Then we go home together. That's a lot of togetherness, maybe more than is fair to ask of any married couple.

When we're writing a musical, I sometimes find myself saying, "That's too much copy; can you distill that?" And she'll say, "Bill, people are not dummies. They can take this."

We have slowly, and not completely, learned over the years that we need to point out each other's strengths rather than each other's weaknesses. We've grown. We've made progress. And we're not as bad in the studio as we were in the early days. Despite my regular resolve to do better, the problem is that I happen to hear harmonics easily, and I think to myself, *This is the lovable human being who is a great mother, lover, and a wonderful wife in all kinds of ways, except she just doesn't hear a harmonic pattern as easily as I do.*

Gloria is aware that many of the people we work with are better singers than we are, and it bothers her. She wants to do better. I tell her, "Honey, it doesn't make that much difference. Singing is not the reason you're here. You're here for who you are, not for what you can do or how you sing."

Whether that makes it any easier for her, I don't know. We're on our way toward thirty years of marriage, and because of working together, it has not always been easy. But there's no one in this world I love more or would rather be married to. I believe our marriage was made in heaven. There are times when other people make demands on me and I just have to call time out and insist that Gloria do the same. When we need and want uninterrupted time together, we take it. Alone together, away from the recording studio and the business and all my Martha duties, we're at our best.

The overwhelming and overarching goal of where we want our lives to go is to have an impact on people for the cause of Christ. Both of us know that it's more important to cooperate on that than to win any argument. Our commitment to each other and our commitment to Christ is strong. On a given day the commitment to Christ is even stronger than our commitment to each other, because as great as each of us thinks the other is, we are not enough for each other. Married couples who think their mates are enough are headed for trouble. Your spouse cannot meet your every need. It's too much to ask. We have promised God that we will love each other forever, and sometimes it is out of dedication to Him that we fulfill that promise.

When we squabble, I get angry with both of us. We're supposed to be effective communicators who have evidently made sense to a lot of other people, and yet we can't make sense to each other! I want to live out at home the principles we write about in songs like this:

I Am Loved

All I had to bring was imperfection;
There was so much more I lacked than I possessed.
I could hardly comprehend His offer:
I'd give all I had—He'd give the rest.
I said, "If You knew You wouldn't want me;
My scars are hidden by the face I wear."
He said, "My child, My scars go deeper;
It was love for you that put them there."

Forgiven, I repeat it, I'm forgiven.
Clean before my Lord I freely stand.
Forgiven, I can dare to forgive my brother;
Forgiven, I reach out to take your hand.

I am loved, I am loved, I can risk loving you,
For the One who knows me best loves me most.

*I am loved, you are loved—won't you please take my
hand?
We are free to love each other—we are loved!**

Gloria is very forgiving and gets on with life, much
better and more quickly than I do. That's one of those
differences that usually favors women. They tend to get
things out and get them off their chests, while men too
often internalize things and wallow in them.

I'll never forget when our dear friend Bob Benson was
on his deathbed in the final stages of cancer. Bob's wife,
Peggy, told him we were there. He was too weak to open
his eyes. He merely raised a hand to acknowledge us.

"Bob," Peggy said, "Gloria says she's going to pout if
you don't let her write that book with you."

I said, "And you know how bad a pouter she is."

Bob smiled weakly, eyes still closed.

"'Course Bill never pouts," Peggy said.

"No," Gloria said. "Not for more than three or four
days at a time."

At that Bob opened his eyes and said in a raspy voice,
"Yeah, he'd probably pout longer if he had a better memory."

CHAPTER ELEVEN

I WISH YOU

*We'd like to collect you and shield and protect
     you
And save you from hurts if we could;
But we must let you grow tall, to learn and to
     know all
That God has in mind for your good. **

*M*aking too much of the difficulty of two intense, independent, creative personalities getting along in a marriage may give the wrong impression. It's only fair to say that Gloria and I truly do complement each other and that our home has been a happy and interesting place for years. Our kids are grown and mostly gone at this writing, and I have to say we're grateful to God for the young adults we produced with His help.

Most of the credit for that, on a human level, is due

Gloria. The world is full of givers and takers, and anyone who knows Gloria knows she is a giver. She has given and given to our children the same way she has given to me all our married life. Whatever the tension and struggles, she has made sacrifices to be and to do what I have needed and wanted her to. My expectations of her have frequently been unkind and not Christlike. Jesus would not have reacted that way. But Gloria kept giving.

Her giving is one of the reasons I love her so much. If she hadn't met me, she probably would have gone on to earn her doctorate in English and would be teaching at some major university. For whatever reason, when I was twenty-seven and she was twenty-two and just out of college, she gave the rest of her life to me—a wonderful gift. I believe she has felt fulfilled by what we have done together and that I have been a liberal husband in encouraging her to exercise her gifts on her own, too.

I have never felt possessive of her or jealous of her gifts and abilities. At first she did not make an issue of finishing her graduate degrees. When we got married and began a family, she felt that raising children was the most important thing she had to do. Even more than the writing, she felt she needed to be a mother to our kids, and she's been a fantastic one. The kids say that too. I think she's been a better mother than I've been a father. She's had more patience.

In general, she thinks I was too tough on the kids, and of course, I thought she was too loose. That sometimes made for conflict, but overall we balanced each other fairly well, as many couples do. The struggle for us was that we had too many full-time jobs. Many songwriters only write music. Many music publishers only publish music. We have done both, plus we have been performers

Bill with his first dog, Popcorn.

Sandlot softball was one of Bill's favorite games as a young boy.

Bill, Danny, and Mary Ann with their parents, George and Lela Gaither.

The house in Alexandria where Bill grew up and where his parents still live.

Bill's first forays into the professional music world were with his brother, Danny.

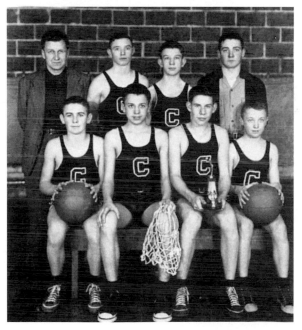

Bill also enjoyed playing basketball in junior high. He's second from the right in the back row.

Bill's high school graduation picture.

Suzanne, Amy, and Benjy get a little help on their homework from Dad.

Bill and Benjy (age 11) having a chat in the rolling pasture outside their home.

The Gaithers spent plenty of time relaxing together
by the creek when the children still lived at home.

Bill's fiftieth birthday party was quite a celebration. Pictured left to right are Bill's father George, brother-in-law Donnie, sister Mary Ann, brother Danny, mother Lela, son Benjy, daughter Suzanne, wife Gloria, daughter Amy, Bill, and mother-in-law Dorothy.

A winter shot of the Gaither house. The land is a special legacy of the relationship Bill's granddad had with the owner.

Bill and Gloria at home in their kitchen, working on new song ideas.

and parents and spouses. I'm not complaining; we *chose* to do all this. Everything we do is related to our overall goal and mission, but it all requires time. Our days were always filled, and if we had not tried so hard to live by our priorities, we could have lost control of the most important things—our kids. I'm grateful to the Lord, and to Gloria, that that didn't happen.

This whole business of the complexity and challenge of raising children makes me a little reserved—maybe even somewhat cynical—when everyone else exults over a newborn. Relatives and colleagues crowd around and coo and gurgle and gush about how cute and beautiful the little thing is. I just smile and nod. "Pretty cute," I'll admit. "Pretty special. Lots of potential." But I'm thinking, *Will all these people be around and supportive and available when this little one becomes a teenager in the blink of an eye and starts questioning everything he's ever heard and challenging his parents every minute? Where will they be when he's fallen into sin or dropped out of life? Will they still think he's cute and adorable and cuddly?* At that time this adoring crowd of admirers diminishes to two people—Mom and Dad. Babies become bigger packages, and those packages sometimes contain surprises for which no parent is prepared. It seems to me we need to aggressively do all we can to build into little minds the stuff of which responsible Christian adults are made.

That's why Gloria and I wrote an album for kids, including this title song:

I Am a Promise

I am a promise, I am a possibility,
I am a promise with a capital "P."
I am a great big bundle of potentiality.

And I am learnin' to hear God's voice,
And I am tryin' to make the right choices,
I'm a promise to be anything God wants me to be.

I can go anywhere that He wants me to go,
I can be anything that He wants me to be,
I can climb the high mountains, I can cross the wide sea,
*I'm a great big promise, you see!**

In spite of my tendency to be tougher on the kids than she, Gloria wrote a line once that beautifully sums up what consistent parenting often is about: "Saying no may mean I've said yes to something higher."

That's a tough truth to convey to a kid, especially when he or she becomes a teenager. Of course, it's hard to convince a teenager of anything! Try telling him he's not going to live forever. Convince him to take care of his body. In this day when there are so many parenting books published, it's scary for an old-fashioned, Protestant-work-ethic guy like me. Experts warn against being too critical of your children's health, hygiene, and lifestyle, and I worry that someday one or more of my children will lament, "I could never please my dad." Those are the kinds of things you hear from maniacs who commit heinous crimes.

At the same time it seems to me that a loving father has to say to a child, "If you keep listening to music at that level, you're going to damage your hearing. If you stay up late and get up late, you're going to develop lazy work habits. If all you eat is junk food, you're going to develop poor eating habits and suffer from bad nutrition."

I never wanted to harp on my kids, and yet neither did I want to neglect them or deprive them of the values I learned. If even part of the success of the Gaither Music Company was due to discipline and hard work, I wanted my kids to know that and to emulate it to their own benefit and the benefit of whatever ministry they chose. Scripture promises that if you train up a child in the way he should go, when he is old he will not depart from it. It doesn't say what will happen in the meantime. I heard a wise, old parent say that his kids hadn't turned out yet, and they were in their fifties!

My assurance to my kids was that there was a major difference between what I said at home, "inside these walls," and how I felt about them when they were out there in the world. As far as Gloria and I were concerned, and we said this more than once, "You couldn't do anything to change our love for you." But we also told Suzanne, Amy, and Benjy that they were going to have to function in a world that was not going to love them just because their name happened to be Gaither and a world that certainly was not as forgiving. In fact, that name might be a strike against them. People might assume certain things about them because they are Gaithers. We pointed out habits we saw developing that were antagonistic and would alienate them from the world and prevent them from becoming all that we felt God wanted them to be. The challenge was to serve up those kinds of helps to our kids in positive ways so they wouldn't leave home frustrated at never being able to gain our approval.

The opposite end of that spectrum would call for being so lenient that your children become brats, self-indulgent to the point where they can't or won't function in the world. It's always gratifying to hear from schools or where our kids have worked, "You've got great children." As with most parents, we're always a little shocked to find that our kids have listened and that they perform better "out there" than they have at home.

It's very popular today to blame our upbringing for all our problems. I remember nothing but firm and consistent love from my parents, but there were also times when Mom or Dad whipped me good and made clear to me, "No, you will not act this way." I needed that. I grew from it. Did it warp me, give me guilt and regret for the way I was raised? Not on your life.

It's a wrestling match raising kids these day, I know. You want them to feel secure and loved, but you don't want them to be brats either. I'd like to see more people emphasize discipline and responsibility in childrearing. We need to trust in the grace of God that we will not turn our kids away from us or from the faith by setting certain standards of holiness for them.

One philosophical rule of thumb we've tried to remember is that it is not only impossible to teach a kid what to think, it would also be wrong if it *were* possible. The best gift we can give our children is to teach them *how* to think. If we give them all the answers, what will we do when they are out from under our influence and the questions change?

We're living in a world where even the vocabulary has changed. When I say Coke, I mean Coca-Cola; the kid of the '90s means cocaine. When I say gay, I mean happy; the kid of the '90s means homosexual. When I say high, I mean the opposite of low; the kid of the '90s means a drug-induced state. When I say bad, I mean the opposite of good; the kid of the '90s means good! Definitions and circumstances change, so if we're only giving kids' answers, when the foundations change, they're out of answers.

The best gift we can give kids is to teach them *how,* not *what,* to think. That goes against the grain of almost any parent. We long to shield our children from all the evil influences of life in the world. But unless we intend to stunt their growth and require them to live under our roofs until they are middle-aged, we do them a disservice.

Gloria and I expressed this the best way we knew how in a 1977 song, and neither of us can quote the crazy thing without breaking down.

I Wish You

I wish you some springtime, some bird on the wing time
For blooming and sending out shoots;
I wish you some test time, some winter and rest time
For growing and putting down roots.

I wish you some summer, for you're a becomer,
With blue skies and flowers and dew;
For there is a reason God sends ev'ry season:
He's planted His image in you.

I wish you some laughter, some "happy thereafter"
To give you a frame for your dreams;
But I wish you some sorrows, some rainy tomorrows,
Some clouds with some sun in between.

I wish you some crosses, I wish you some losses,
For only in losing you win;
I wish you some growing, I wish you some knowing
There's always a place to begin.

We'd like to collect you and shield and protect you
And save you from hurts if we could;

But we must let you grow tall, to learn and to know all
That God has in mind for your good.

We never could own you, for God only loaned you
To widen our world and our hearts.
So, we wish you His freedom, knowing where He is
*   leading,*
There is nothing can tear us apart. *

Eventually letting go of your children does not have to be so hard. If they are happy, it's easier. If a kid is troubled and you're unsure of his character or the solidity of his foundation, then you worry and the empty-nest syndrome hits hard. Of course, empty-nesting is difficult for Gloria anyway, precisely because our kids were such a joy and she misses them. But I have to think letting them go would be even more difficult for her if they were at loose ends besides. She has always been a nester who enjoyed having the chickens in the roost. I enjoyed it, too, but since she was better at it than I, it's only natural that I accept the empty nest a little easier than she does.

For me the good thing about the kids' being gone is that I get more time alone with their mother. It isn't that I was jealous of the time they required or that I don't want to see them as often as I can now, but our life together was much different as a family than it is as a couple. It's fun to be back to just the two of us, dating, courting, and investing hours in each other. My challenge now is not to let the business get so cumbersome and time-consuming that all the hours freed up by having the kids gone are reinvested there at the expense of our

*Words by Gloria Gaither. Music by William J. Gaither. Copyright © 1977 by William J. Gaither. International copyright secured. All rights reserved.

marriage. We have looked forward to these wonderful years.

I wouldn't trade those years of child-rearing for anything, but part of me is glad they're over and that the kids are doing well. I wouldn't feel so good about it if they all still wanted to live at home or came back to escape bad marriages. It's harder to keep your fingers out of their lives when they are struggling. Eventually you realize that you must let them work themselves out of tight situations so they will develop the muscle to do it again in the future, much like a butterfly in a cocoon.

The greatest rewards to us as parents come when our children reunite at our home. That's when we're grateful we didn't succumb to the temptation to move. A few years ago when everyone came back for Benjy's twentieth birthday cookout, Amy said, "I forgot how much I love this place." What could more warm a parent's heart? It's impossible to express how important it is to stay in the same place more than two decades and plant trees, to see them grow, to remember where we used to sled down a hill and now see it covered with trees. It seems to me that if you build a kid's memories of happy, wonderful, warm family times in a place he can come back to and remember, his chances of straying too far will be pretty slim.

When the kids come back, I want them to notice the relationship their mom and dad still have. I want them to see and know that we are honest with each other, that we say what we think, that we try to be kind and loving and giving and forgiving. They still need the security of a solid marriage, even when they are away and on their own and married themselves. We continue to work on our relationship because, just like the Christian life, a marriage does not stand still; it either grows or stagnates.

Businesswise I'm heading more in the direction of

withdrawing than expanding right now. The biggest motivation for that is that I do love my wife and would like to spend more time with her without wrestling over business decisions. She has always been an important part of the business, and she pretty much knows everything that's going on. She's one of my closest advisers, which isn't always easy because we don't always agree. Making the business less and less important to our own relationship has to bring benefits.

If you and your spouse ever disagree, join the club. Don't hide, don't pretend, don't camouflage your true feelings under the notion that you're being kind. Your anger will explode someday in some other form and infest your home with poison. Embrace life. Embrace grief. When you lose a loved one, grieve as hard as you can. When you fight, fight tough. When you argue, argue loud. Love hard, cry hard, live hard. There's health in that.

Gloria and I got married because we believed God wanted us to, and He knew there would be struggle involved. I believe the world's a better place because we're married. We brought three beautiful people into the world, and I like to think we created a lot of wonderful babies in our songs. I've never doubted that ours is a special union.

Relationships have their ups and downs, their deserts and their oases, their winters and springtimes. I can't tell you the joy of getting through another hard Indiana winter and looking forward to being outside with Gloria, the person I love the most. Something inside me says to hang in there and wait it out and the snow and ice will make me enjoy the springtime even more.

We all go through hard winters in our lives, but there's always the promise of spring.

Thank God for the Promise of Spring

Though the skies be gray above me,
And I can't see the light of day,
There's a ray breaking through the shadows,
And His smile can't be far away.

Though the earth seems bleak and barren,
And the seeds lay brown and dead,
Oh, the promise of life throbs within them,
And I know Spring is just ahead.

Thank God for the promise of Springtime,
Once again my heart will sing;

There's a brand new day a-dawning,
Thank God for the promise of Spring. *

CHAPTER
Twelve

LEARNING TO LOVE
THE FAMILY OF GOD

Warming myself by the fires of His Spirit,
Camping right close to His throne . . . *

*B*ecause I'm a down-home kind of guy, I want people to feel at home with me and with our music. I want them to enjoy themselves and feel blessed, worshipful, excited about Jesus and leave believing they have been in the presence of the Lord.

Despite that wish, we have been on the receiving end of criticism through the years. Call me overly sensitive, too much of an "artiste," whatever you want, but I answer all negative mail personally. I have to tell you, in nearly three decades of ministry and thousands of pieces of mail, we have been much more encouraged than discouraged. It has been gratifying to see how people express their love and support, and I'm thrilled that we have been able to have such a positive impact on so many people.

When we do get criticized, I take it personally, as well I should. What we do is what I direct, and I'm happy to take full responsibility for the package. Interestingly, of all the critical mail we have received, I would estimate that only about 5 percent has been in the area of substance. Most of our critics are upset by questions of style.

When I first started I knew I had to be straight on my theology because theology is important. And there are many people within the church who would rightly and meticulously comb my lyrics for doctrinal purity. Fine. We should all be careful in that regard. But style, musical expression, is so subjective that you can't win. Sure, there are safe, mainstream, middle-of-the-road Christian artists who have a wonderful, warm, easy style that a broad cross-section of listeners loves. Performers who try to in-novate will reach some of the people some of the time, but never all of the people all of the time.

Sadly, many in the church have made monuments of our worship forms. We have raised our ebenezers (a pile of rocks indicating a place where God had met with Old Testament people), as the old song says, but nowadays there are lots of *new* ebenezers. Yet people generally resist change. They forget that just because God met someone in a special place once doesn't mean that's the only place He will ever meet them. We have worked like crazy all our lives to try to help people see the living God in a variety of musical packages, and too often people respond nega-tively to the style and miss God.

At a National Religious Broadcasters convention in the

early 1970s, Ralph Carmichael, John W. Peterson, and I were on a panel that was to once and for all solve the age-old question, "What kind of music is God's music?" Does it surprise you to know that they've posed the same question a few times since, with three different guys on the panel?

Even the three of us who discussed that issue have distinctive styles and approaches. I respect and admire and love those guys, and each has his place in the broad spectrum of godly music. Some people love what we do and don't care for what the others do, and vice versa. That's fine. Each to his own. But to judge someone's spirituality or motives because his music evokes something negative for you? That's not right.

Back in the 1940s John W. Peterson wrote one of his first musicals, and by his own admission it was influenced by Broadway melodies. He used interesting and fresh progressions and octave-and-a-half ranges. He told me he received a letter from a well-known pastor who scolded him for "sending a bunch of kids down the wrong path by putting Scripture to such secular music."

John told me the letter was so strong that he couldn't get it out of his mind for thirty years. Then, in the early 1970s when the contemporary Christian music scene began to change dramatically and quickly, that same pastor wrote to John again. He said, "I can't believe what's going on in Christian music today. Whatever you do, John, hold the line."

What a classic example of the truth that we have this heavenly treasure in earthen vessels, and though the vessels change, the treasure will never change. The gospel is the same yesterday, today, and forever, but its packaging keeps changing.

I have my own preferences, styles that appeal to me more than others. But I've lived long enough to know that when a message is meaningful and changes lives, it shouldn't really matter to me what wrapper it comes in. Not long ago I heard a good message in a song by a secular pop artist in a style I didn't particularly care for. But he was singing about something he wished he had expressed to his father during what he called "the living years." It was a wonderful truth, and I realized that if I had been simply hung up on the fact that stylistically it wasn't my cup of tea, I would have missed a wonderful message.

Learning to handle criticism has been a career-long chore for me. Many artists insist that they do not read their critics, but I doubt that's widely true. Most would likely be as sensitive as I am, and as I often tell my staff, "We can learn from our critics."

However, there is a right way and a wrong way to express a concern. A wonderful, positive way is to encourage and to state your problem forthrightly without questioning motive or intent. People who begin their complaints by accusing us of striving for a bigger audience or more money can get our attention, but naturally that puts us on the defensive. They have questioned our hearts, and if we truly believe our motives are right, we are now hurt and insulted and less receptive to what otherwise might have been a legitimate complaint.

Once we came back from a weekend when I felt God had invaded our Friday night concert in a very real way. It was one of those occasions when I could feel the visitation of the Holy Spirit. The evening was wonderful and the experience beautiful. The next night the same thing happened. We were in Seattle so, knowing that we could not get back to our home church the next day, we accepted a Sunday night engagement as well. For the third evening in a row, we felt we'd been in the presence of God. I don't know how good the music was, but we had given it all we had and God had done the rest.

We got home very late Sunday, and when I finally got into the office Monday, I enjoyed going through the mail and finding many affirming letters of encouragement and appreciation for our ministry. Of course, it would be a few days before such letters reached us from Seattle, but I was still basking in the glow of those experiences and enjoying notes from previous concert attendees.

Then I came upon a letter from a man who had heard us on an evening that I thought had gone well. To him the public address system had been too loud. He didn't like the way we had dressed. He didn't like the style of the music. And he didn't like what he considered my misuse of humor (Well, at least he recognized it was humor. Some don't.)

I like to have fun at concerts, and sometimes I even poke fun of my own penchant for stammering when I get excited or tired. And sometimes it even happens on stage. When it does, I tell the apocryphal story of selling Bibles door to door when I was in college. My approach was, "M-M-My name is B-B-Bill Gaither. D-D-Do you wanna b-b-buy this Bible or d-d-do you w-w-want me to r-r-read it to you?"

Anyway, this man found nothing he liked about our concert and gave it to me with both barrels, especially attacking my motives. Through the years there have been only a few letters I have thrown away. If they are so unreasonable and vitriolic that I know there will be no reasoning with the writer, I toss them. I did not put this one in that category. I laid it aside and thought about it for a couple of days.

My first reaction, naturally, was anger. I felt defensive. I wanted to tell the man what I really thought, but my letter would have been no better than his. There have been times when I have immediately dashed off a response, but upon re-reading it have thrown it away, knowing that the Lord would never send that kind of letter.

Two days later I was still upset about the letter, so I gave it another day before I finally responded:

Dear Sir,

I came in Monday morning after a wonderful weekend of concerts in Seattle. On Friday and Saturday and Sunday nights we enjoyed thrilling services where God invaded our world in such a way that it made me feel proud about what He had called me to.

My Monday morning mail brought lots of confirming letters. A few people had constructive criticisms, but they were shared with a sweet spirit. They said things like, "Next time I wish you'd do this," etc.

Then I came to your letter, and it really threw me, because you attacked my motives in a very detailed, critical, and—I felt—harsh way. First, I was angry and put it aside, hoping I had misunderstood it and that it would be clearer later. I thought, *Maybe he didn't really mean that*.

I read it again later and still didn't want to answer it because I would have responded in a spirit of anger. Now, three days later my anger has passed, but my pain remains. I don't know what your intent was, but I have to tell you that all the good things that happened last weekend have been clouded over by your letter, and I still can't come up with a positive answer for you.

The night you were criticizing, we did as well as we

humanly could. That was as good as we can do what we do. All I can say is that if your intent was to hurt me or dampen my enthusiasm for our ministry and what we're trying to do for the cause of Christ, you succeeded. The last three days I have not written any songs or done very much constructive because your letter has been on my mind.

I am really sorry we didn't meet your need. Forgive me. I love you and God loves you.

> Sincerely,
> Bill Gaither

I never heard from the man again, which was probably just as well. Some years ago, however, I did hear back from a woman who had written a critical letter. She said she had tuned in our New Year's Eve program, "Jubilate" at the Omni in Atlanta, which we did live before fourteen thousand people and broadcast over television.

To be honest, technically the broadcast was not done as well as I would have liked, especially the sound. The artists were great—Sandi Patti, Carman, BeBe and CeCe Winans, our trio, our vocal band, and the Cathedral Quartet—but it was the first time we had tried to televise such a big event. We had sound problems and a few other glitches, simply because we were not prepared to translate the excitement of such a huge undertaking to an intimate medium like TV. The people who were there had a great time and wrote us nice letters. However, the woman who watched on television was not happy, but not for the technical reasons I would have imagined. She wrote:

> I have followed you for years and loved what you have done, but I tuned in "Jubilate" for twenty minutes and I was appalled. It looked like show biz. The Bill Gaither

Trio is not the same old group that I used to know and love.

I wrote her back:

> I received your letter and am very sorry that we disappointed you. We knew people would be flipping the dial that night, and we wanted to get their attention. There were things we did to try to reach a secular television audience that we wouldn't normally do. We wanted to tell them in a very powerful way that Jesus Christ was the answer. We were hoping that if they were out there watching at midnight and were depressed and down, we could grab them with a highly energetic program and then get our message across.
>
> We love you and care about you, and we appreciate your interest in us over all these years. I think we're the same group we've always been. We're doing things in a little different way, but it's in the same spirit and it's the same people you knew at the beginning.
>
> Before you totally write us off, please do me a favor. I'm going to send you our latest record [which at the time was "Praise Gathering: An Evening with Bill and Gloria Gaither and Their Friends"]. It was an evening of praise, the type of thing Gloria and I have been doing for years, and we used various young artists. I think it's a wonderful record and I want to ask you to listen to it all the way through one time. If you then still feel the same way, at least we have tried. We still love you and want you to pray for us. I just wanted to make this one last attempt before I lose a friend.

Within ten days I got a letter back from her:

> Thank you for your response and the spirit of it. Forgive me for my quick reaction and the harshness of

my letter. I kept a copy and re-read it and realize I was too quick in my judgment. You are right. I listened to the record and I was in tears. You are the same group I knew and loved.

The bottom line? The critical man accomplished what he set out to do. The woman responded as a true sister in Christ and thanked us for being sensitive to criticism. We do learn from our critics. People are not bad because they come across as angry, hurtful, and harsh. They generally react to things that are important to them.

The apostle Paul admonishes us, however, to speak words of encouragement to the brethren. There's nothing so heartwarming as a letter of encouragement, and I don't know of a better encourager in my life than Billy Walker of the Billy Walker Evangelistic Association in Detroit. We sang a few times for him back in the early days, but as our organization started growing and we could no longer accept those engagements with him, he had two alternatives. He could have said, "Who do they think they are? They've gotten too big for us," or he could have become supportive.

He became a supporter. Whenever we're in the Detroit area, Billy is there in our corner. And it's rare that I don't get a most encouraging letter later. He'll write: "Once again, you did it, Bill!" I know we happen to ring his cultural bell, being right where he is musically, but the fact that he takes the time to say so means the world to me.

Such long-term friends and supporters make me feel responsible and make me want to continue to be vigilant. I try to surround myself with people of integrity who really know me and know that our goal is to be ethical and upright and pure. I'm not a perfect person, as anyone who lives with me or works with me knows. But I also take a great deal of comfort in the fact that the people who have been with us the longest and are the closest to us are the ones who trust us the most. Our friends, office staff, and accountant are the ones who truly know our motives and intentions. They know where our hearts are, because they work with us every day.

One of these days we will stand before God and be held accountable for our relationships. We are to live our lives in an honorable way so as to encourage others in the Lord. I feel responsible for my secretary of more than twenty years—Carolyn Hall—for my business associates, for my wife and my children. Sometimes an employee will tell me, "My husband thinks you're the greatest, so if you had a few minutes, could you encourage him?" That's a heavy responsibility. What it tells me also is that what that husband thinks of me is based on what his wife has told him. That's humbling.

I try to protect myself and my integrity by belonging to a small group of men that has met for several years, sometimes for prayer but always for accountability. We keep each other honest. It's been helpful to get together and talk about the things that concern us. I recommend it to any man; it's nice to have people around you who love you and care about you enough to say, "You know, that doesn't make sense to me." They force you to rethink your positions and defend your opinions. It's healthy and good.

Our group began when I started getting together with Don Collins, chaplain at Anderson University, and a couple of other guys just to talk about issues of the day and things important to us. The more we did it the more we enjoyed it, and now the guys make it a priority. We'll juggle other things on our calendars, but not the dates and times of those meetings.

I also have some close personal friends that I consult on a one-to-one basis about sticky issues. I may be dealing with a delicate ethical or moral matter with another artist. I seek advice from these close friends who have proven they can keep confidences, and it has been a huge benefit to me.

It's all part of wanting to keep my feet on the ground, not to begin believing the press releases. I thank God for the gifts He has given me, but that doesn't make me any better or any more important or any more significant than anyone else in the kingdom. We all do well to remember that and to keep in contact with people who aren't afraid to remind us.

There's no room in God's kingdom for a "superstar" mentality. We are called to be humble, like our Master. Jesus warned his disciples, "Whoever desires to become great among you, let him be your servant" (Matthew 20:26). We are called to join the family of God on equal footing.

Plenty of Room in the Family

Plenty of food at the table,
No need to economize there;
There's all you can hold and there's plenty besides,
And the storehouse will never be bare.

There's lots to be done in the family,
A job to fit every man;
There's caring and lifting and loving to do,
So pitch in and help all you can.

If you're lonely and looking for friendship,
If you're lost and you want to be found;
There's plenty of room in the family of God,
And there's plenty of love to go 'round.

Plenty of room in the family,
Room for the young and the old;
Plenty of happiness, plenty of love,
Plenty of room in the fold. *

CHAPTER THIRTEEN

CHANGES

If neither foes nor loving friends can hurt you,
If all men count with you, but none too much . . .

—Rudyard Kipling

---

*F*riends, especially older ones, help keep your life in perspective. If you don't keep it in perspective, life will sooner or later eat your lunch. Long-term friends are the most precious kind, and I'm especially blessed to count several in my life. The late Bob Benson was a special friend, as are Bob MacKenzie, Wayne Buchanan, Fred Bock, Ronn Huff, Jerry Weimer, Randy Vader, Bob Rist, Wayne Erickson, and the list goes on. We have many friends in our business and at Anderson University, and I realize it's unusual to have so many who could truly be considered close.

Part of a good, happy, fulfilling life is the ability to make and maintain friendships and keep good relationships. I appreciate so much my friends who honestly understand that, because there are no perfect people, neither are there any perfect friends. I want to be a good friend, but I don't want anyone to expect me to be perfect. That's not friendship; that's pressure.

We human beings can be wonderful; we can also be jerks. Once we understand that, we are free to develop friendships that can last years. Too many of us were raised in the church in a manner that makes us tend to categorize people. There are the believers and the unbelievers, the Christians and the non-Christians. But also within the church there are the good people and the bad, the trustworthy and the not. Some people are considered *in* because they've stayed married and raised a family. Other people are treated as outcasts because even though they are Christians, they are divorced or were once caught in some "big" sin. I believe in and advocate holy living, but something bad happens if we draw too fine a line and demand perfection from people. What we have done is to disparage the forgiveness and restoration God Himself offers. When we become so black and white in this area, our list of good guys shrinks. Someone disappoints you, shows some selfishness or anger or pride, and he's out. The problem is, on a given day, any of us can be bad guys and disappoint one another.

An associate of mine met a guy he was really impressed with. He built this guy up to me every time he talked about him. A year later he had nothing but horrible things to say about the man. "Can I tell you something?" I said. "The guy you described to me a year ago as someone who could do no wrong was never really that great or fantastic. And the guy you're describing today is not that bad and evil. He's probably like you and I are, somewhere between those extremes."

As I grow older I find myself more eager to hang out with those who are honest and understand me and admire my good qualities and who also try to bring out the best in me. They are the ones who understand that I have bad days, that I may sometimes make unsound judgments, that I make mistakes. Fortunately, these relationships do not falter when I blow it.

Many of my long-term friends have come from the music business, which is also unusual, because many business relationships go sour. Most people would not be friends if they weren't capable of working together. But I have friends I'd rather not work with. If my problem with them was morals or ethics, then no, I couldn't be their friend either. Those are not in question. Sometimes friends are simply strong personalities who clash too often in business situations. It's better for some friendships that they remain social and relational rather than contractual.

One thing I can always count on my friends for is honesty, a rare commodity today. If I'm right that a true friend is one who will be honest enough to sometimes tell you what you need to hear and not what you want to hear, it's easy to distinguish between new and old friends. Frankly, I trust my life-long friends more than the ones who have come along in just the past few years. New friends may become long-term friends, but that takes time and patience and trust.

My personal challenge is to be the kind of friend that I want to have. Sometimes ignoring a friend's faults or poor judgment is the easiest route, but what kind of a friend would I be if I didn't say something? If I expect my friend to be honest with me and hold me to a high standard, I need to be willing to do the same. That can hurt. It's tough and painful to confront, but done in love and strictest confidence, it shows true love and friendship.

When I first heard Waylon Jennings and Willie Nelson's country hit "Old Friends," I nearly wept. The word picture of old friends pitching pennies in the park is touching and poignant. It makes me realize how fortunate and wealthy I am in that regard because most people say you can count your truly close friends on the fingers of one hand. I would need a couple of extra hands, and I'm talking about people who care very much about me and who I care very much about. We keep in touch.

I also happen to believe that the sign of a healthy male is an ability to have appropriate female friends. I got a note recently from Laura Lee Oldham, Doug's wife, who mentioned that she had just been thinking about me and praying for me. Gloria and I·have known the Oldhams for thirty years, and we used to live in the same town. She said she remembered the days when I used to stop in and have a cup of coffee or bring Suzanne by when she was just a little girl. How much is it worth to get a note like that from an old friend? It cannot be calculated.

It has been a tremendous asset for us over the years to run with Fred and Lois Bock, Wayne and Sue Buchanan, Bob and Joy MacKenzie, Bob and Peggy Benson, and Wayne and Jan Erickson. Our families were intact, our marriages not without problems but solid, our priorities fixed. How many children could say their parents had four other close sets of married friends like that? We all cared about each other and were interested in what was happening with each other's kids. We were all like surrogate aunts and uncles to them, thinking about them, talking about them, praying for them, counseling them.

Unless there is something I don't know about, I can point to those people and say here are some friends who are very human and very earthy and certainly don't live with their heads in the sand, yet they have affirmed in subtle, yet strong ways, that marital faithfulness is their only choice. These friends are models of fidelity.

I still have a buddy from high school I meet often when I'm home to go over to the track and reminisce. That's not only physically healthy, but it's also psychologically healthy. I wouldn't trade that relationship for anything. In times of crisis I have several people I can turn to. A lone ranger is in danger these days. When Gloria is away I sometimes have dinner with my good friend Dr. Robert Reardon, and we'll go to Indianapolis for a ballgame. What perspective it gives me to sit and chat with a man in his seventies. Older guys are extremely helpful in the maturing process because no matter what you're going through, they've been there. Too few of us take advantage of that kind of counsel and input when the older men are still around to provide it.

If you can develop only one friend in your life, by all means, go for it. If you find yourself as fortunate as I am and can list several, count yourself blessed. No one should attempt this Christian journey on his own, and we all need to reach out, if for no other reason than to discover who's on the road with us.

Getting Used to the Family of God

Going together, enjoying the trip,
Getting used to the family I'll spend eternity with.
Learning to love you, how easy it is,
Getting used to the family of God.

Reaching our hands to a brother that's new,
Learning to say that I really love you,
Learning to walk as the Father would do,
Getting used to the family of God.

Climbing the mountains, crossing the plains,
Fording the rivers, sharing the pain;
Sometimes the losses and sometimes the gains,
*Getting used to the family of God. ***

I suppose one of the reasons I put so much emphasis on longevity and older friends is that I'm aware of the passing years. Our audiences have changed because we have changed. When we began ministering I was in my late twenties. Our friends were young married people with small children, and our audiences were the same. When we spoke and sang about raising a family in those days, the truth was fresh from the griddle.

Now we and our friends and—for the most part—our audiences are twice that age. We should be singing, "How sweet to hold a newborn grandchild!" We still try to reach young people, but we'd be kidding ourselves if we thought people of a new generation would rather hear us than Carman or Sandi or Amy. Those artists will mature with their audiences too. If we tried to become rockers to guarantee a younger following, we'd be laughed off the stage.

Many friends and supporters tell us, "You guys are just as powerful and effective as ever." Well, that's nice to hear, and there are times when I'd like to think we're still as widely influential as we once were. But time has moved on, and I'm at peace with the role the Lord has given us

*Words by William J. and Gloria Gaither. Music by William J. Gaither. Copyright © 1974 by Gaither Music Company. International copyright secured. All rights reserved.

today. If we are still influential, it's because we've been instrumental in bringing younger artists into the limelight, sharing our platform to help launch them. In that way we are still associated with cutting-edge, contemporary Christian music.

It's critical that we not get caught up in thinking we are "successful." Kipling's point applies so often. Apparent success or failure in this life is not the issue. I take comfort in believing that God honors consistency. Though we may get weary in doing good, we are to keep doing what we know is right because sooner or later—usually much later—it pays off in eternal rewards. The good coach gets his job done in training camp so that during the season he only has to make mid-course corrections. You don't pass a test by cramming the night before. You just keep doing your job, don't panic, and stay in the pocket.

That lesson, learned slowly over a long period, has also helped me keep in perspective a variety of other issues, such as awards, musical preferences, and cultural differences. Everything is relative and everything changes, except the substance of the Word of God. If we could somehow keep our eyes on that and learn the difference between theological absolutes and cultural preferences, we'd all get a lot more done for the kingdom. I don't adapt to modern culture just to be hip. I simply don't want something as precious as the gospel to be lost by confining it to a style whose time is past.

I've spent an awful lot of my professional life trying to answer letters and be kind to people who have been unkind to me in their criticism of us for "being so sacrilegious as to put a wonderful Scripture like 'We are persuaded that neither life nor death . . .' into a contemporary setting." We got tons of mail on that.

Almost all the criticism we have received through the years has come from people who have misunderstood what we were trying to do from a stylistic perspective. They use words like *worldly, ungodly,* and *unspiritual.* I always want to hear people out and give them the benefit of the doubt, but one thing I'm confident of is that our messages and lyrics are anything but what those critics say. The messages come from our devotion to Christ, from our prayer life, from our time in the Word, from living for Him in this world. All I'm trying to do is communicate something very important to as many people as I can. Yes, a wider audience is one of our goals, but not for the purpose of financial gain. I am simply trying as hard as I can to make the biggest and widest impact I can with the truths I believe are important.

Probably the toughest call for anyone in Christian music is drawing that fine line between art and ministry. When Handel's *Messiah* is performed, is it art? Is it ministry? To some it's only art. Every Christmas many people sing Handel's *Messiah* who don't know the Messiah, simply because they see the music as great art. By the same token, there are people who sing it as a wonderful form of worship and praise to almighty God. To them it is only ministry, because maybe they can't even carry a tune. Others, of course, see the piece for what it is, both ministry and art.

How about contemporary Christian music? When a kid goes to an Amy Grant concert, is it art or ministry? To some it's just art. To others it's ministry. Does that make Amy bad? No. She's doing what she does as well as she can do it. As long as her motive is right before the Lord, and I believe it is, she's doing a good thing. (A few years ago she came by to record a few lines for us, and I remember she couldn't stay long because she had promised to baby-sit for her sister's kids. I told her, "Amy, always keep those kinds of priorities, and you'll do just fine.") When our ministries cross the line and become only art for art's sake, then there's a problem.

But how do we define that problem? Is the problem our methods? Is it our tools? Is there a problem because we use microphones, speakers, guitars, keyboards, spotlights, just like secular performers? I don't think so. That's only a problem when the style and the vehicle become the message. That's when technique gets in the way of content, which is death in any art form—preaching, painting, singing, playing, writing, you name it.

The only way to keep that from happening, especially when you have a group of highly talented musicians, is to keep focused on why you do what you do. If people like a certain guitar lick or a high note or a crescendo, the temptation is to play to that. Then you start enjoying the doing of it and the response you get from it, more than you enjoy praising the Lord with your talent.

When I feel oppressed by what I consider nitpicking, I remind myself that the church once went from songs such as "Then Jesus Came," which was a wonderful gospel song basically without rhythm, to "In the Garden," which had a waltz, three-four time. People wrote the publisher and said it was evil because you could dance to it! When you think about it, "Victory in Jesus" is in four-four time, and you could do a can-can to that!

We all draw the line somewhere for our own personal preferences. Even young rockers have limits on what they enjoy. I may not like a certain sound, but I'm not prepared to throw out the whole message with it or to question the motives or the spirituality of those who understand that sort of music.

I do think the current pop culture has gone about as far as it can go as far as wild styles and appearances. Obviously, they can't get any louder. There's medical evidence that this generation's hearing has been impaired already. I have cautioned young people to be careful that they don't permanently damage their ears. This is also a danger for engineers who spend a lot of time in the studios, regardless of the type of music they produce.

On stage we don't do anything close to heavy metal, but we do have some tunes that are rhythmically pretty energetic. To some people that's too much. Our plea is that our critics would look past the form to the content, to the lyric and its message. They'll find that we remain with our roots.

We Are Persuaded

We are persuaded that neither death nor life
Nor any other power from below or on high,
Things in the future or in days gone by
Can separate us from His love.

If God is for us, who can be against us?
And who condemns Him, by God's own Son has been
*   forgiven!*
By hope we're driven, by grace forgiven;
We're called by purpose to be spent for service.

His resurrection takes imperfection;
And through our weakness, His mighty power is
*   speaking.*

In pain there's singing, in death no stinging;
Of this we're certain: through everything His love is
*   workin'!**

Being "called by purpose to be spent for service" means just what it says. If we can remember that and not get our heads turned by praise or criticism—which are just as much impostors as success and failure—we'll be on our way toward keeping life in perspective. The applause of men is a heady, often delightful thing, but it should never be the reason for our work.

CHAPTER FOURTEEN

GET ALL EXCITED

I'm excited about a solution for the world;
I'm gonna shout and sing . . .[*]

*D*uring a string of years the
Gaithers won a lot of awards and I was named songwriter
of the year, but the business of awards needs to be kept in
perspective. I believe there is validity in honoring people
who have contributed something to the Christian community. But it becomes a problem if an artist's whole year
begins to revolve around award week, wondering
whether he won or lost. By now you know my philosophy of winning and losing, so I suppose it depends anyway on who's keeping score.

I never begrudge someone a well-deserved honor. I

love some of the Songs of the Year from the recent past. People often ask me if there are songs I wish I'd written. There are many. I always rejoice over the success of a good song, regardless of who wrote it. One of my favorites is Jack Hayford's "Majesty." I appreciate the lyric and the tune and the way it builds. It's a beautiful expression of worship and truth. I have also always loved Andraé Crouch's "Through It All."

Gloria and I have had the privilege of introducing artists to the broader Christian community simply because we knew they had something strong and unique to say and that they would do it in a powerful, effective way. That can be dangerous. Some people, like Sandi Patti, are naturally going to be accepted because of their talent and force and because they sing in a style widely accepted by the mainstream. Carman is outrageous and funny and had some rough edges at first, but he really speaks to the younger crowd and adults as well. Don Francisco stretched our audience as far as it could be stretched at that time, but he won them over because of his depth and content.

I suppose I'm as gratified at Don's eventual acceptance as with anyone's, because when we first took him on the road, audiences were skeptical. Here was this long-haired kid with a guitar, wearing jeans and sandals, sitting on a stool and singing a powerful song about the resurrection from Peter's perspective. With a rough, primitive, driving narrative style, Don would slowly take the wary crowd with him into Peter's prison cell, describing the apostle's feelings about walking with Jesus. He recounted all the things they did together, and the fact that now Jesus was dead and gone. Then He appeared and Peter went out into the streets screaming at the top of his lungs. I can still hear

Don doing that at the top note of his range: "He's alive! He's alive! He's alive and I'm forgiven! Heaven's gates are open wide! He's alive! He's alive! He's ALIVE!"

People wrote and said, "When I saw this long-hair come on stage, I wondered what in the world Gaither was trying to cram down our throats now."

Others wrote, "I'm sorry. I just thought you were trying to sell more tickets and reach more people. But at the end of the song I was sitting there with tears in my eyes, wondering what had happened to me."

I admit it: From the beginning Gloria and I have tried like everything to push back people's cultural preferences—their barriers, really—as far as we could. We wanted to say, "See? You're shortchanging yourselves on truth! There's a lot of truth coming in packages that can dramatically change your life if you will just listen to it."

I'll never forget when we introduced the Second Chapter of Acts at the Praise Gathering. The group consists of a brother and two sisters, and the brother, Matthew, has hair as long and beautiful as his sisters'. To be honest, at first I was concerned. I was hoping people would see past his appearance. They did.

It was the last night of the Praise Gathering and, sure enough, there was some skepticism when Second Chapter appeared. The wife of a business friend in his sixties told me later that he muttered to her, "What's Gaither trying to pull?" But after Matthew sang a simple, beautiful, high, and clear rendition of "My Jesus, I Love Thee," the woman told me her husband just wept.

My Jesus, I Love Thee

My Jesus, I love Thee, I know Thou art mine—
For Thee all the follies of sin I resign.

My gracious Redeemer, my Savior art Thou;
If ever I loved Thee, my Jesus, 'tis now.

I love Thee because Thou has first loved me
And purchased my pardon on Calvary's tree.
I love Thee for wearing the thorns on Thy brow;
If ever I loved Thee, my Jesus, 'tis now.

I'll love Thee in life, I will love Thee in death
And praise Thee as long as Thou lendest me breath;
And say when the death dew lies cold on my brow,
"If ever I loved Thee, my Jesus, 'tis now."

In mansions of glory and endless delight,
I'll ever adore Thee in heaven so bright;
I'll sing with the glittering crown on my brow,
"If ever I loved Thee, my Jesus, 'tis now. *

That is fantastic. That is what Jesus is all about. Only He could knock down the cultural walls in this generation. Someone else told me he was critical of our using Second Chapter of Acts, "But I gotta tell you, we were having a tough time with our son until I heard that young man sing. I realized we don't all have to look alike to still be devout and love the Lord."

When Gary McSpadden started with the group, he was a younger and different kind of vocalist. Larnelle and Michael were also unique, and we changed some as they came on board. But we never tried to be something we weren't. If we think an idea may be limited by an extreme style, we'll try to adapt only up to a point. The ideas remain more important to us than the way we present them. I have been impressed to hear Billy Graham use more hu-

*Words by William R. Featherston.

mor during recent years, probably to keep an entertainment-oriented audience's attention long enough to feed them heavy ideas.

Where we get controversial and run into problems is with people who are married to the culture, not in a modern, worldly sort of way, but people convinced that God speaks only through a particular style of expression that happens to coincide with their generation. If they grew up in the 1920s, then certain forms of dress and music, even color and modes of expression, are considered godly. Others are considered worldly. If the '50s was their era, all those perspectives change.

When some of the secular music we now consider cute and bouncy—like Dixieland or rag—first became popular, it was denounced by the church as too associated with dance halls and saloons. As those people get older, that same music reminds them of their childhoods and becomes nostalgic and sentimental; then the gospel can be packaged in it, but even then, only that older generation likes it. See the irony? When they were kids, they were taught that this kind of music was evil. Now they accept it as part of their childhood, but they want it to carry Christian truth. They don't want the younger generation using its own styles and modes of expression.

Of course, this judging of people happens between musicians all the time too. It's easy to screen others' work through our own grid of preferences. Any musician who looks down his nose at any other musician is doing a dangerous thing. I have always loved the simplicity and beauty and doctrinal purity of Fanny Crosby's work, yet it's not uncommon to hear more sophisticated musicologists sniff at her work as if it is juvenile or simplistic. Theologians might say she overemphasized relational theology in songs like "Blessed Assurance," but tell that to the millions who have been blessed time and time again by that great gospel song.

People criticizing a Fanny Crosby song remind me of the old story of the tour guide in Europe who was showing a masterpiece painting. A tourist said, "I don't see anything so great about that." The guide replied, "Sir, the painting is no longer on trial; the viewer is." Fanny Crosby is no longer on trial. Not everything she wrote was a masterpiece, but those that have stuck, those that have moved generation after generation, prove the critics wrong.

People often ask me about songs I wish I had written. I said I loved "Majesty" by Jack Hayford. I wish I had written Don Francisco's "He's Alive," Stuart Hamblen's "This Old House," Annie Johnson Flint and Hubert Mitchell's "He Giveth More Grace," and Lanny Wolfe's "Greater Is He That Is in Me." But I don't love these songs only because they've become popular. I appreciate them for the positive effect they've had on my life and walk with the Lord.

Of my own songs, I particularly like "I Am Loved," because most of the people I know who are uptight about life don't really believe they are loved. My very favorite among those I've written tends to vary from day to day, but I keep coming back to "It Is Finished," simply because I think there's good theology and sound psychology in it.

Of course, there are other artists and songs I admire artistically, although I may not agree with everything they stand for. We don't have to agree with everything a person says or does to appreciate his or her work. We should be able to separate that very easily. I happen to like much of John Denver's music, but obviously there would be many areas where we would disagree philosophically. But then the man who made my suit may be as far from the cross of Christ as anyone I've ever met. The people who own your local grocery store may be pagans. We need to choose our issues to fight over and start looking for ways to draw people into the kingdom, rather than building walls to keep them out.

I've been influenced musically by many artists. I grew up in a country home and was exposed early to ballads. To me one of the greatest songs ever written was Hank Williams's "I'm So Lonesome I Could Cry." So emotional. So moving. So clearly from the heart.

I listen to a little bit of everything. Though I came out of that country background, in college I got into classical music. People shake their heads when they see the tapes in my car. I might have a Gatlin Brothers album right next to a Rachmaninoff. Somebody once told me I must be the most musically eclectic person he had ever seen. I take that as a compliment because I am not into a style; I'm into the message.

I told people at a seminar in the late 1970s that I like Anne Murray, the Gatlins, Neil Diamond, and John Denver, and an older gentleman stood with a question. "Isn't there a danger that if you keep listening to stuff like that you'll take away the uniqueness that endeared us all to you back when you started?"

I said, "Interesting you should say that, because the Bill Gaither you knew and loved back then was not just Bill Gaither. He was all of the influences that had been poured into him up until then. When my mother was bathing me behind the pot-bellied stove on a Saturday night in Indiana and listening to the 'Grand Ole Opry,' I was hearing those sounds. And later, the classics and even the Ames Brothers ['You, you, you. I'm in love with you,

you, you,' and 'We'll have these moments to remember'] were poured into my psyche. When I was nineteen and became a Christian, those sounds were still there and played a part in the type of music I write to this day."

People still want to know where the anointing of God begins and ends. If styles are interchangeable and amoral, where do you draw the line on the art package as it relates to communicating the Christian gospel? I draw the line at the place where the performer ends up receiving more attention than the Lord. Obviously, he has to get the attention of the audience to communicate to them, but not for the sake of his own adulation. When the concert is over and the performer has been the primary focus, Jesus gets lost and is not honored. That is not an anointed presentation. That's where I draw the line. Whether it's a classical keyboard artist who gets caught up in flipping the tails of his coat or the rock band who's so carried away they'd rather be doing secular stuff, you've got a problem.

Rather than list groups I do or don't care for, I think that principle (keeping the attention where it should be) is the best way to determine who is worth listening to. I have no problem with a song that excites a crowd about the Lord and even helps them take that excitement to the streets to make a difference in the world. That's why we wrote and we still sometimes sing:

Get All Excited

Get all excited, go tell everybody
That Jesus Christ is King,
I said, get all excited, go tell everybody
That Jesus Christ is King,
I said, get all excited, go tell everybody

That Jesus Christ is King,
Jesus Christ is still the King of kings, King of kings!

You talk about people, you talk about things
That really aren't important at all;
You talk about weather, you talk about problems
We have here at home and abroad;
But, friend, I'm excited about a solution for the world,
I'm gonna shout and sing and it's
Jesus Christ is still the King of kings, King of kings!*

There's a big difference between being doctrinally careful—which I believe in—and drawing lines so fine between denominations and cultural preferences that we paralyze ourselves for service. Before I get into a doctrinal argument with someone, I always want to know first whether it affects the way I live. Now, if you want to talk about something like repentance, then yes, that's worth talking about. If a person doesn't understand genuine repentance and godly sorrow for his sin, then he will be like the drunk who says, "Sorry, I did it again," without ever turning from his bad habits. Is he sorry enough to die to the sin of drunkenness and leave it behind, becoming a different person because of that experience? Or is he willing only to say, "Help me! Give me something, medication, anything to get rid of my guilt"?

I know that only God's work through the Holy Spirit brings true change in people; it isn't the work we do by repenting or turning that changes our lives. But somehow we have to get back to the place where we are held to a standard and expected to live up to biblical principles, not to earn our salvation, but to show gratitude to God for it.

*Words and Music by William J. Gaither. Copyright © 1972 by William J. Gaither. International copyright secured. All rights reserved.

CHAPTER FIFTEEN

TAKE TIME TO BE HOLY

Take time to be holy, be calm in your soul—
Each thought and each motive beneath His
    control.
Thus led by His Spirit to fountains of love,
You soon will be fitted for service above. *

*H*oliness is a passé concept
even with the church today, but the scriptural admonition
to live holy is still there. Such living is most threatened in
the life of a musician when his priorities get out of whack,
when he treats success as a given instead of a bonus, or
when he forgets about grace and graciousness.

If you program your mind in the beginning to focus on
ministry, and you maintain that focus, then if material,
temporal, human success comes, you just thank God for it
and stay focused. When you start aiming at success as its
own reward, you're in danger.

*From "Take Time to Be Holy" by William D. Longstaff and George C.
Stebbins.

I remember when all we had to do was whisper we were coming to town and ten thousand people would show up. That was a bonus. We knew then that this would not always be the case. Just as it was important not to start assuming we were popular and successful because we were so wonderful, it's important to realize why.

Above all, I want to handle with dignity and grace both those success and failure impostors, our highs and our lows. This period now of maturation I see not so much as a shifting of impact. One exchange for aging is giving up mass appeal. It goes with the territory and it happens all the time. No artist should ever be seduced by the numbers because the numbers aren't always right. The message we communicate on stage today is probably more valid and solid than what we were doing when we were thirty because some measure of wisdom comes with maturity.

We're saying the same basic things we were saying decades ago, but now, because of our experience, we've refined those things so that they hit and apply more powerfully. Finally, merely because we've lived long enough, some will say, "Okay, I believe you now." When they—and we—were in our early thirties, they might have said, "Wait, withhold judgment. Wait 'til he's lived a while. See if he still believes what he's saying twenty years from now."

It's tough for a group of college singers to come to a church and start telling the old saints how to live. The congregation will usually smile and nod while thinking, *We'll wait and see how you feel about all this twenty or thirty or forty years from now.*

There are some benefits of aging. One is that some people will listen now who didn't before. There is credibility with longevity, as long as your life has been consistent and you've been able to live out those things you've espoused through your music. Gradually, your art has become deeper ministry by virtue of the sheer amount of time you've spent developing the talents you're given.

When we're on the road we usually have about fifteen people on stage with us. I'm sure they get tired of my calling them all around before the concert every night and hearing me say, "Focus, focus. Why are we doing this? Let's remind ourselves again why we do this." In the meantime, we joke around and have fun and do all kinds of exciting music, but what are we aiming toward? What do we want to happen? I use various techniques to get everyone's head and mind into what we're doing. One night I simply said, "Let's pray," and didn't close until the usually vocal ones had finished praying and there had been enough awkward silence to start bringing out some of the others.

When you wait, you are often rewarded. From here and there came heartfelt prayers from some who had always let someone else do the praying in the past. And the longer I waited, the more open and sincere and vulnerable the prayers became. Soon people were confessing bad attitudes, frustration, impatience, homesickness. Something was happening. We were getting our eyes on Jesus, and God was pointing out our failures. We were drawn close in a special way, and the concert that night was one of the best we'd had in a long time. How much better that is than a hastily called minute of prayer where somebody thanks God for the opportunity and asks Him to bless us. That's okay, but it's not enough. We have to be broken before Him and focused on our purpose.

It does take time to be holy and to give God a chance to intervene in our lives and the lives of the audience. Just because our business is communicating doesn't mean we should do it—even if we could—without God. Turning technique into ministry should be done with fear and trembling because we understand the awesome responsibility and tremendous privilege that is. If we forget that and live for the applause of other human beings, we'll wind up emotionally bankrupt anyway.

People are fickle. I sat at a National Basketball Association all-star game one year with my friend Norm Sonju, general manager of the Dallas Mavericks, and heard the whole crowd yelling "Michael! Michael! Michael!" for Michael Jordan. Norm turned to me and said, "Bill, people are pretty fickle, aren't they?"

"Why do you say that?"

He pointed down about ten rows to a balding, middle-aged man sitting by himself. "See that man?"

"Yeah."

"That's Bob Cousy, probably the best guard who ever played this game. Nobody's yelling his name or hounding him for an autograph."

If you're living on applause, you won't live long. The wild cheering of the audience will fade quickly and completely.

One year, Gloria was asked to say a few words at the Dove Awards, the annual ceremony where the Gospel Music Association presents its honors for best record, best artist, and all the rest. The organizers wanted her to put into perspective what the Christian music ministry is all about. It's not about bloc voting to get certain artists and companies to win. It's not about fancy clothes and a glittery show. Christian music is about ministering to people and either drawing them to Jesus or inspiring them to give themselves more completely to Him.

Gloria never takes such assignments lightly, and she was prepared that night. We'd had several performances and music of all styles before she was introduced. She was greeted with enthusiasm, but the place quickly fell silent as she began:

> We're here to honor excellence tonight, and I suppose that's okay. Jesus had a lot to say about excellence and greatness. He said that the greatest in the kingdom was the one who would lay down his power, take a basin and a towel, and wash another's feet.
>
> Peter didn't understand it then, and most of us do not understand it now. But Jesus still says, "He who would become a master must first become a servant."
>
> There are many unsung heroes in our field who will not get an award here tonight, but they are great because of many "behind-the-scenes" deeds of kindness. There are those who have spent many personal hours working and have spent a lot of personal income helping the disenfranchised of our society. Many of them have been involved in street ministries, missionary work, soup kitchens, homes for unwed mothers, etc. Many times, it has gone unnoticed here, but it was heard like a voice of thunder in heaven. They spelled out in bold letters once again what it is we are all about.
>
> Thank God for their contribution to the kingdom.

When she finished, the audience heard a simple off-stage piano introduction as a choir stepped into place. From behind the curtain strode George Beverly Shea, who sang in his straightforward yet majestic style. As soon as the capacity crowd recognized the song, they began to applaud, and they applauded throughout the solo.

I'd Rather Have Jesus

I'd rather have Jesus than silver and gold,
I'd rather be His than have riches untold;
I'd rather have Jesus than houses or land,
I'd rather be led by His nail-pierced hand;

I'd rather have Jesus than men's applause,
I'd rather be faithful to His dear cause;
I'd rather have Jesus than worldwide fame,
I'd rather be true to His holy name;

He's fairer than lilies of rarest bloom,
He's sweeter than honey from out the comb;
He's all that my hungering spirit needs—
I'd rather have Jesus and let Him lead

Than to be the king of a vast domain
Or be held in sin's dread sway!
I'd rather have Jesus than anything
This world affords today. *

The people were applauding not just the example of Bev Shea and his eighty years of saintly, humble living. They were applauding the truth of what Christian music is, or should be, all about. They were saying, yes, this is important. This is why we do what we do. I want to be able to say from my heart that I'd rather have Jesus than any award. And that relationship requires my time.

I was reminded of one of the great songs of the faith that would have been just as appropriate had its author been there to sing it.

Little Is Much When God Is in It

In the harvest field now ripened
There's a work for all to do;
Hark! The voice of God is calling,
To the harvest calling you.

Does the place you're called to labor
Seem so small and little known?
It is great if God is in it,
And He'll not forget His own.

Are you laid aside from service,
Body worn from toil and care?
You can still be in the battle
In the sacred place of prayer.

When the conflict here is ended
And our race on earth is run,
He will say, if we are faithful,
"Welcome home, my child—well done."

Little is much, when God is in it!
Labor not for wealth or fame;
There's a crown—and you can win it,
If you'll go in Jesus' name. *

So what happens when what you're doing for Jesus results in applause and success? Accept it as a bonus and be grateful. I'm grateful for everything. I'm thankful I'm part of the human race. I'm thankful God loved me enough to send His Son to die for me. I'm thankful that after I gave up the dream of performing, God gave it back to me when my motive became to change lives, not to

*Words and music by Kittie J. Suffield. Public domain.

177

show off. I'm thankful that though writing was my new mission, performing was a bonus and that any success or accolades were exciting extras.

Anybody in music is thrilled when someone likes what he or she is doing, says it's wonderful, and is even willing to support it financially. Sometimes they write letters telling you how something you wrote or sang or said was powerful enough to make a change in their life. That is very affirming and nice, but I can say honestly that even then, something down inside me says, "William, this is a bonus. This is not going to be this way forever. Give thanks for it. God has blessed you. Be a good steward of the resources. Don't take it for granted."

You don't go through life jumping from mountain peak to mountain peak. The fact that there are peaks means there necessarily have to be valleys. The best singer in the world could release the greatest-selling record of all time, and the next time out, even if his effort is the second-best ever, it will not measure up to the first. No one soars at the same level forever.

That's something to remember. It is very difficult for human beings, once they get power, not to use and abuse it. But look back over your life and you'll find that the times you grew and matured were not when you were winning big and wielding power. The growing times came when you were down and losing and hurting. You were vulnerable. It was painful, but you grew. And that's why I maintain that only time will tell if a win is really a win or a loss is really a loss.

I would guess that a very small percentage of all Christians would choose to lay down power that was at their disposal. Jesus was the supreme example. Look at the power He had and what He chose to do with it! He not only laid it down, but He allowed Himself to be killed in spite of it.

Power brings pride, and pride will do you in as quickly as anything. A woman came up to a young singer and told him his was the most beautiful voice she'd ever heard. He said, "Oh, it wasn't me; it was Jesus."

She replied quickly, "Oh, no, you weren't *that* good!"

It's stupid for anybody in the Christian field to get too prideful because it's simple: The Lord giveth and the Lord taketh away. I treat any gift I have pretty carefully, realizing that tomorrow it could be gone.

Not by Might, Not by Power

You may pressure men and sway them to your view;
Your words may make them do what you want them to
    do;
You might make your money talk and throw your weight
    around,
But without the Spirit of Jesus, you are just a clanging
    sound.

You may have bombs enough to blow up all the earth,
Arm a million volunteers and keep them on alert;
You may have power and might to make men fear and
    quake,
But if you lack what God demands, you've made one big
    mistake,

Because it's not by might, not by power,
But by my Spirit, saith the Lord.
It's not by might, not by power,
But by my Spirit, saith the Lord. *

With all the experiences in our lives and career, I can look back on the earliest days of what most people would call our successful years and say that a pivotal decision there influenced our future more than anything. We had been traveling to Nashville so often to record that we decided it would be worth our while to build a good studio near home so we wouldn't have to be away from the kids that often. So, we began building Pinebrook Studio. It became the main place for our recording and allowed us to spend a little more time at home. This gave us more time to focus on the more important parts of life: the Lord and our family.

Then we found ourselves working for many different sponsors and promoters, some good and some not so good. We learned a lot the hard way. We organized Spring House, a concert promotion company that would do things right, so we—and anyone who used the service—would know what kind of quality to expect when they showed up at a concert. We also developed a copyright administration company, and all of a sudden we were a little conglomerate. All I had wanted to do was write songs and sell records and sheet music, and now we were responsible for seventy-five employees. It became tougher to manage our personal lives well.

One might think that I was this little small-town poet and composer longing to be an entrepreneur and a great administrator, having to worry about payroll, insurance, and executive decisions. I wasn't. I had to learn a lot of things the hard way. But the Lord was good to me, and gave me the grace to handle the tough days.

After a few years in the business of managing people, I know more than I ever thought there was to know about managing resources, being thrilled with people, being disappointed, being a leader, being a discipler, and being a model. And I've also learned about trying to live a holy life before the Lord, in the public eye. Because of His blessings, I believe both the business and my personal life have been worthwhile. And I hope the lessons I've learned can help you in some way.

CHAPTER
SIXTEEN

BROKEN AND SPILLED OUT

And though You were perfect and holy,
You gave up Yourself willingly;
And You spared no expense for my pardon—
*You were spilled out and wasted for me!**

*T*here are those who might believe that building a company can make a man somebody. He could, I suppose, create his own empire and get people to do his will. But by trying to run my small company by biblical principles, I have found what a humbling thing it can be.

When I think that all I wanted to do was get my music out to a broader audience, I marvel at what's become of the Gaither Music Company. I used to handle the day-to-day administrative stuff myself. Now I have executives who run the various divisions, and I basically try to give them room.

Sometimes I give them so much room they don't feel they know what I want. I'm a typical artist, I guess, who has little business trying to run an organization. But that's why I have trusted people in important positions. I think they're all quite good, and for the most part they think I could improve on communication.

Ironic, isn't it, that a man who has made a life and ministry out of communicating to the masses frustrates his own executives by being too busy or too deep in thought to keep them as informed as he should? When I started this business, all I wanted was to write good songs. Now selling my songs has become managing accountants and marketers and publicity people and everything else that we've been blessed with. Sometimes when I pull into the parking lot of the company, I identify with the writer of the old pop song who said, "Look what they done to my song, Ma. Look what they done to my song."

I'm a very self-critical person, probably a perfectionist. Sometimes when I come backstage at intermission our various technical people will say, "Boy, Bill, it's really going well," and I say, "No, it's not. Here's what I'm unhappy with." I've had people say, "I feel really good about what's happening out there tonight," and inside I feel like a scratch golfer who's shooting ten over after nine holes. I'm not playing for other people's approval. I'm not competing against other performers. If I'm competing, it's against a standard I know I should be striving to reach.

I know that I should simply do my best to the glory of God. Yet in a way, that is how I do my best. I want every detail to be right. I want the light and the sound and the tuning and the timing just so. There are enough distractions and enough amateurish ways of communicating. I want what we do to be special.

I want to keep high standards for the business too. Our overarching principle is to run the business the way Christ would. I'm not perfect, obviously, and I haven't hired anyone who is, but Christlikeness is the target we shoot for. It's not easy. But striving for that ideal makes for certain prerequisites, like how we treat people. People become more important than products and profits. Employees are to be regarded as more important than we are. The executives are to have servant attitudes, which is not always convenient and never automatic, but it's always kind and right.

Servant-leaders lead by asking questions. I spend a lot of my time asking not, "*How* do we do this?" but rather, "*Why* are we doing this?" The true leader is comfortable with the word *why*. Good employees should be comfortable with that question too. It's almost as important to hire servant-workers as leaders, and we have been very fortunate in that regard. I hope it reflects Gloria's and my attitude that we have a lot of hard workers. People who join us evidently are willing to labor intensively. Many people look at our industry and believe that anything having to do with the arts is mostly fun and games. We do have fun. But we also work hard.

Many of the people who have worked for us over the years have gone on to places of important responsibility elsewhere. I'm proud of that. If we're doing our job well, we ought to be producing some whole human beings who are out there doing a good job somewhere else.

There are days when I look in the mirror and at our executives and staff and wonder if we just can't find people anymore with Christlike attitudes. But that's no time to give up. Even though we are sometimes not the best models, we have a teaching and a discipling responsibility. We're to hang in there as Jesus did with the twelve imperfect, childish, selfish, sometimes dastardly human beings He chose to work with. He lost one traitor in the process, but with the remainder He built a magnificent kingdom that will last forever and ever. Yet even He said, in essence, "How long must I put up with you?" When we deal with people with short attention spans, we have to remind ourselves of Jesus' frustration at His sleepy disciples ("Could you not watch with Me for one hour?").

An old friend of mine, Rocky Snowden, told me when we first began to build our organization: "Bill, one thing you'd better come to grips with, in dealing with people, is being content with long-term results. If you expect too much too soon, you're going to get discouraged and decide it's not worth it." That's been valuable advice. When I hear someone criticize someone in our organization, I remind them, "You have to understand, I'm looking at a continuum. Yes, I see and have a desired end, but I also see the point from which that person has come and thank God for how far he has already come."

Sometimes we do have to sit down with someone and get serious about moving him farther along that continuum. There are even times when righteous anger is okay. I've had a young associate with whom, a few times over the last dozen or so years, we've sat across the table and gone at each other with high emotion. Every time, somewhere in the conversation, I remind him, "I have a feeling you're not going anywhere, and I know I'm not going anywhere. We're gonna continue to work for the cause of Christ and His kingdom in a brotherly way. Right now we have to hammer this out because neither of us feels good about it."

That's what true relationships are all about: long-term commitment to stick it out, just as in marriage. You're not going to have a good marriage or a good business relationship in which you don't have two strong-willed people going nose to nose once in a while.

Most of the leaders in our organization are as strong-headed as I am, and I wouldn't have wanted them around if they weren't. But that also produces times of healthy and intense conflict. Our arguments are never because one wants to do something bad and the other something good. That would be too easy. Anyone could make that call. If someone wants to do something morally, legally, or ethically wrong, he won't be around here long. Our conflicts arise when two people have differing opinions of how to do something right. We have had to learn to submit to one another and compromise sometimes. Letting go of your pride can be very difficult.

No matter where we go or whom we are with, we represent Jesus, and our attitudes—on and off the stage—have to reflect that. It's both gratifying and painful to hear promoters and sponsors in various towns compliment us on how easy it is to get along with the people in our organization. It's gratifying because we want to be easy, as far as our personal needs are concerned. We have high standards and demand a lot of devotion to the work, yet we strive to put our personal comfort second for the sake of the ministry. What's painful about that is that people's reactions make it clear that most artists, even Christians, are demanding. You expect that from secular groups with their special contract clauses for imported foods and beverages, separate hotel rooms for each individual, all that. But when a Christian artist demands star treatment, something is awry. It's one thing to insist on a certain level of technical excellence in the equipment and certain amenities that make the program work, but it should not be the responsibility of the local sponsor to make the musicians' lives luxurious.

The more we get treated like royalty, the more we enjoy it, get used to it, expect it, and eventually demand it. Gloria and I fight that. Of course, we appreciate every kindness, and it does help to have others looking out for you when your mind is on a million concert-related details. But I want to model to our people that no one should be above carrying equipment. At my age and station in life, I'm sure no one would raise a critical brow if I went from the stage to the bus and relaxed while the crew packed and loaded the equipment. But am I really more important than those people? I can't justify that biblically.

I carry equipment, not to shame anybody or to show off my humility. I do it mainly because of my work ethic, but also to get going. I want to get home. I don't have to yell at someone for being lazy or playing the star if I'm the owner of the business and I walk past him carrying a speaker; he can see what's wrong for himself. People who insist on being served all the time miss the joy of finding out what life is all about.

This business of being patient with people for long-term results carries outside our company, yes, even to people who have ripped us off. Anyone who's been in business for any length of time has been treated unfairly by someone. It's happened to me, and I don't mind being open about it. I think part of hanging in there is remaining consistent despite the setbacks. Some will say, "I can't believe you still do business with so-and-so and treat him well after he has misused you."

I try to return evil with good because I know it's the

right thing to do. Of course I'm not the type to get walked on for long without learning a lesson. But if a guy does me wrong, even on purpose, I'm willing at some point down the road to give him another chance. After all, we're all made up of a bunch of pluses and minuses, and nobody's perfect. It's all part of living in brokenness before the Lord.

But there are others who have made my life more enjoyable too. I don't like to get into names, even on the wonderful side of the ledger, because there are so many I could list, but one of the most Christlike people I know is Buddy Greene, a bluegrass virtuoso. It's so hard to find minuses in his life that I've told him, "Buddy, you make the rest of us look bad." His reactions are always good. In many ways he reminds me of a collie, so loving and forgiving. Gloria and I have two mature collies now, but when they were puppies I remember walking into the kitchen and accidentally stepping on one of their tails. He yipped, then immediately licked my foot, as if to say, "You didn't mean it, did you?" I told Gloria, "What a wonderful example of grace! Wouldn't it be wonderful if everyone in the world reacted like that when they got hurt? To say, in effect, 'I know you love me and mean to do me good.'" Buddy is one of those types. I met him through Bob MacKenzie, who said, "Bill I've got a musician you'd really like. He plays harmonica, he's a bluegrass musician, and just the kind of a guy you'd take to." Mac was right. As soon as I heard Buddy, I said, "Let's do something together," and he started traveling with us. He had come to the Lord as an adult and wanted to use his music for God. He had played in Jerry Reed's band, and so he came with a lot of experience and credentials. He matured quickly in the faith.

Not only did I find a wonderful musician friend who makes a great contribution, but I also found a born teacher and Christian leader. He's the guy who—when I'm not around to do it—will call the rest of the group together to tell them about a verse of Scripture he's found meaningful. It would be great if all of God's children were like Buddy, but they're not. I'm not, and I wish I were. This relatively new Christian has passed up the veterans in instincts and sensitivity and motivations and reactions.

For instance, sometimes when you program an evening, something goes wrong and you realize halfway through the concert that something has to be cut. I look back at Buddy and say, "Hey, I'm not gong to be able to include your third song," and he immediately says with a smile, "No problem."

I wish more artists acted like that. Many might pout or even get angry. They might say, "You had time for all your songs and your comments and your corny jokes, but not for my number." And they will often be right. It will have been my fault. An artist has to have a fairly healthy ego to even get up in front of people and do his thing, so few will react with as much humility as Buddy. Ironically, it's hard sometimes not to take advantage of him, knowing that he is the one artist who will roll with the punches. What an attitude! What a deep well he must draw from.

You never know how people are going to react until you get them in the heat of battle. I've had them stomp out and promise it was their last night with us. Not Buddy. Fire only makes him shine. He's got the kind of attitude reflected in this song written by Bill George and Gloria, made popular by Steve Green:

Broken and Spilled Out

One day a plain village woman,
Driven by love for her Lord,
Recklessly poured out a valuable essence—
Disregarding the scorn.
And once it was broken and spilled out,
A fragrance filled all the room,
Like a pris'ner released from his shackles,
Like a spirit set free from the tomb.

Broken and spilled out just for love of You, Jesus,
My own precious treasure, lavished on Thee;
Broken and spilled out and poured at Your feet—
In sweet abandon, let me be spilled out and used up
    for Thee.

Lord, You were God's precious treasure:
His loved and His own perfect Son,
Sent here to show me the love of the Father;
Yes, just for love it was done!
And though You were perfect and holy,
You gave up Yourself willingly;
And You spared no expense for my pardon—
You were spilled out and wasted for me!

Broken and spilled out just for love of me, Jesus,
God's most precious treasure, lavished on me;
You were broken and spilled out and poured at my
    feet—
In sweet abandon, Lord, You were spilled out and used
    up for me. *

*Words by Gloria Gaither. Music by Bill George. Copyright © 1984 by
Gaither Music Company and Yellow House Music. International copyright
secured. All rights reserved.

CHAPTER SEVENTEEN

IT IS FINISHED

A battle is raging for the gain of man's soul or his loss.

I thank God for grace because without grace I wouldn't have a friend. Who would put up with my idiosyncrasies? I'm not the easiest person in the world to get along with. I'm impatient. I have a short fuse. Thank God there are people who have extended grace to me. I have to be willing to do the same for them and for everyone with whom I come in contact.

The body of Christ, the family of God, is a place where you can fail and still not be a failure. No matter how many times you think you've failed, there is still grace at the foot of the cross where you can start again and be whole. Now, we can give ourselves to the idea that it's always been like this, that we're from a long line of failures and so nothing will ever change, or we can be willing to fill the shoes of the good and godly examples of those who have gone before us.

When we learn to live in the world and not become part of it, we will have made a major step in the direction of becoming good role models ourselves. But as Christian men deal with this all-important question of balancing the Mary and the Martha priorities, as we carefully evaluate Kipling's two impostors, triumph and disaster, as we strive to keep calm and stay in the pocket without panicking or scrambling, we're neither in the world nor out of it. We're not of the world, but we're worldly in our thinking. We're materialistic, but are we doing anything to change the world?

Let's admit it: Those are the issues that eat our lunches most every day. Tennessee Ernie Ford sang, "Sixteen tons, and what do you get, another day older and deeper in debt. St. Peter, don't you call me, 'cause I can't go; I owe my soul to the company store." We owe our souls to whatever is driving us. The true life struggle is keeping a balance between the company store (Martha stuff) and what's really important (Mary stuff). There have been enough songs, poems, and slogans reminding us to stop and smell the roses, but we seem to think it means everybody but us.

Can you really do this, and if so, how? Does it involve turning over a new leaf, talking to your spouse and deciding on new priorities, changing your lifestyle, getting organized? A very successful friend told me recently that he is cutting a lot of overhead out of his life—dropping out of a club, selling a lavish home and luxury car—saying, "These things are not worth it." He said he had found himself a slave to all that.

I've tried hard not to let our overhead dictate our artistry and ministry. That's not easy because sometimes you're forced to cut good programs that are helping people. But if a man is doing his job well, he should be working himself out of a job. There's no reason to keep all the activities and commotion going forever. Some things in life are just more important than others. At each stage of life, you have to reevaluate all the busy-ness in your life against what you *need* to be doing to be the person God wants you to be. Give up the frantic rushing around. Give up the merely "interesting" for the truly valuable. What a simple way to uncomplicate your life!

One wonderful thing about growing older is that whatever new thing comes up, in some way or another I've seen it before. With that feeling of *deja vu* comes the ability to think it through, to keep cool. "Peace, Be Still" is what we call our "peace/therapy" song we have the crowd sing with us. In this day, when we are *all* dealing with high levels of stress, we need to act on our belief that the living Christ is at our side with His hand on our shoulder saying, "Son, Daughter, don't panic. Take My peace. Take My peace. Take My peace."

As I look at the overall problem of the world's crowding out our spiritual values and wonder what to do, I realize that some are being faithful and need to just keep doing what they're doing, in spite of success and in spite of failure. Christ would have us stay in the pocket because that's where He is. We're in the hollow of His hand.

For me to stay in the pocket now, as I move through my fifties toward my sixties, I need to keep a grip on who I am and what my gifts are. Just as when I was nineteen and had to assess them, I must do the same now. What can I contribute? What is the most meaningful thing I can do for the cause of the kingdom? Those who have followed us for years would probably say, "Oh, just keep singing and writing," but there are better singers who can reach wider audiences. Loyal fans say, "There's only one of you." That's flattering, but truthfully I think I can help other people do what they do at this stage of my life and career better than to keep being the one out front.

There aren't enough people grooming the next generation. Too many enjoy their moment in the sun, and then they fade and that's it. I believe strongly in the discipling mandate, that we are called to mentor those who come behind us. Otherwise, we have taken our cut out of the center and have missed our real calling and our biggest blessing. That's sad.

I wrestle daily with the future and where I want to see myself in a few years. I am a planner, a control-type person. It's hard to say how much longer I'll sing and perform on stage. It is still a joy, and there are people of all ages who still say they love our approach. So, as long as I can carry a tune and keep up with the pace of the road and have enough talented people on the stage to help, I'll probably do it. I think helping others perform—as a recognizer and putter-together of talent—is better than doing it myself.

It's been a good life and I've enjoyed it. I hope I've got a few good years left. As I look back I realize that sometimes I've won, sometimes I've lost, sometimes I've gotten rained out. Most of the time I didn't know the real outcome until years later, but it was always part of my nature to stay in the pocket, for that very reason.

When we've dealt with people in counseling situations, I've often said, "Why don't you unclench your fist? Why do you keep re-fighting these battles? They've been won on the cross and you can't win them anymore."

If there's any one thing I would want to characterize my ministry, it's the finished work of Christ on the cross. We have tried to espouse many causes within the body of believers over the years, but our whole purpose has been to point people to Calvary.

It Is Finished

There's a line that's been drawn through the ages,
On that line stands an old rugged cross;
On that cross a battle is raging
For the gain of man's soul or his loss.

On one side march the forces of evil.
All the demons and devils of hell;
On the other the angels of glory,
And they meet on Golgotha's hill.

The earth shakes with the force of the conflict,
And the sun refuses to shine;
For there hangs God's Son in the balance,
And then through the darkness He cries:

"It is finished," the battle is over,
"It is finished," there'll be no more war;
"It is finished," the end of the conflict,
"It is finished," and Jesus is Lord!

Yet in my heart the battle was raging.
Not all pris'ners of war had come home;
They were battlefields of my own making
Didn't know that the war had been won.

Then I heard that the King of the Ages,
Had fought all the battles for me;

And the victory was mine for the claiming,
And now, praise His name, I am free.

"It is finished," the battle is over,
"It is finished," there'll be no more war;
"It is finished," the end of the conflict,
"It is finished," and Jesus is Lord!*

EPILOGUE

Someone once said you have to learn from other people's mistakes because you'll never live long enough to make them all yourself. Well, I've lived long enough to make more than a few mistakes, and I was determined to learn from my own.

Not long ago, Gloria and I carved out some time to get away together, just the two of us. No friends, no family, just us. We went to St. John's Island where no one knew us. On the way down there I read the edited manuscript of this book. As I studied the story of missing the sunset, I made up my mind to be sure I had learned something in this process. I determined that I was not going to miss one more sunset.

Gloria loves the water, so she was in her element. What a beautiful place! We kidded that the biggest decision we had to make every day was where to have dinner. We spent most of each day at the beach, snorkeling, swimming, jogging, or just exploring or shopping in town. When we returned late in the afternoon to get ready for dinner, I made my one call back to the office. If the place was still standing and the staff and loved ones were still living, everything else could wait. The first day I didn't call back at all!

On the third day I teased Gloria because she made *three* business calls! She writes and speaks, and certain arrangements just had to be made, but it was fun to chide her about letting the Martha things get in the way of our Mary experience.

We had a wonderful time together! The unspoiled beaches, nature in nearly its original state, the memories that are still fresh. . . . Some years ago, Gloria wrote a book with Shirley Dobson on making memories. That's what we were doing. One evening we ate at a quaint little restaurant downtown that looked like a place Ernest Hemingway might have enjoyed. It was dark and woody and intimate, and outside it seemed surrounded by foliage.

As we relaxed over an early dinner, knowing we had plenty of time to enjoy the sunset and be back to our room before 9 P.M., I told Gloria, "We should feel guilty being able to enjoy each other this much."

It all culminated in the sunset each night. I felt so fortunate, so blessed to have Gloria's whole attention, and I know she felt the same. Back home we rarely get those uninterrupted moments, let alone days at a time.

God's beautiful handiwork in the sky each evening and the stimulus of the water and sand and wind and each other imprinted images in our minds that can never be forgotten. God had a good idea when He created sunsets. They focus your mind and spur you to think of those ethereal things that make up more of life than we Martha types like to admit.

I shudder to think I once was so busy I almost missed the sunset. Never again.

Beyond the Sunset

Beyond the sunset, O blissful morning,
When with our Savior heaven is begun;
Earth's toiling ended, O glorious dawning—
Beyond the sunset when day is done.

Beyond the sunset, no clouds will gather,
No storms will threaten, no fears annoy;
O day of gladness, O day unending—
Beyond the sunset, eternal joy!

Beyond the sunset a hand will guide me
To God the Father, whom I adore;
His glorious presence, His words of welcome,
Will be my portion on that fair shore.

Beyond the sunset, O glad reunion
With our dear loved ones who've gone before;
In that fair homeland we'll know no parting—
Beyond the sunset forevermore. *

*A*BOUT THE AUTHORS

Bill Gaither is one of the most successful and most honored artists in the history of contemporary Christian music. In more than thirty years as a pianist, composer, and producer, he has received two Grammys, seven Dove Awards, and the first Gold Record ever awarded to an inspirational album.

His creativity has resulted in such standards as "Because He Lives," "The Church Triumphant," "Something Beautiful," "The King Is Coming," "He Touched Me," and "There's Something About That Name." Bill still lives in his hometown of Alexandria, Indiana, with his wife and collaborator, Gloria.

Jerry B. Jenkins' writing has appeared in *Reader's Digest, The Saturday Evening Post,* the *Chicago Tribune,* and dozens of Christian periodicals.

His biographies have included books with Hank Aaron, Walter Payton, Meadowlark Lemon, Orel Hershiser, Joe Gibbs, Mike Singletary, and Nolan Ryan. *Out of the*

Blue (with Orel Hershiser) was fifth on the *New York Times* bestseller list.

His fiction includes *Rookie, The Operative,* several series, and a book of short stories (*The Deacon's Woman and Other Portraits*).

He is Writer-in-Residence for the Moody Bible Institute of Chicago and lives with his wife and sons at Three Son Acres, west of Zion, Illinois.

THE GAITHERS: AWARDS AND HONORS

1968–74

- ASCAP Gospel Songwriter of the Year, Bill Gaither
- ASCAP Gospel Song of the Year, "Because He Lives"

1969

- Dove Award, Gospel Songwriter of the Year, Bill Gaither
- Grammy nomination for Best Inspirational Performance, "He Touched Me"
- Grammy nomination for Best Performance, "He Touched Me"

1970

- Dove Award, Gospel Songwriter of the Year, Bill Gaither
- NEFF, Best Trio, The Bill Gaither Trio

1971

- NEFF, Best Trio, The Bill Gaither Trio, "Back Home in Indiana"
- Dove Award, Song of the Year, "The King Is Coming"

1972

• NEFF, Best Trio, The Bill Gaither Trio, "Because He Lives"
• SESAC International Award for American Composer with the Greatest International Exposure, Bill Gaither, "He Touched Me"
• Dove Award, Gospel Songwriter of the Year, Bill Gaither

1973

• NEFF, Best Trio, The Bill Gaither Trio, "Live"
• Grammy Award for Best Album, "Let's Just Praise the Lord"
• Grammy Award for Best Inspirational Performance, "Let's Just Praise the Lord"
• Dove Award for Gospel Songwriter of the Year, Bill Gaither
• Honorary doctorate degree, Anderson College, Bill Gaither

1974

• Dove Award for Gospel Songwriter of the Year, Bill Gaither
• Dove Award for Gospel Song of the Year, "Because He Lives"
• Grammy Nomination for Best Album, "Thanks for Sunshine"
• Grammy Nomination for Best Inspirational Performance, "Thanks for Sunshine"
• ASCAP Gospel Song of the Year, "Because He Lives"

1975

- Dove Award, Gospel Songwriter of the Year, Bill Gaither
- Dove Award, Best Mixed Gospel Group
- Grammy Award for Best Album, "Jesus, We Just Want to Thank You"
- Grammy Award for Best Inspirational Performance, "Jesus, We Just Want to Thank You"
- General Assembly and Executive Council of the Church of God (Anderson, Indiana) Award for The Bill Gaither Trio's "invaluable contributions in composing, playing, singing, recording, and producing gospel music"

1976

- Highest award from the American Indian Association, "God's Songbird," Bill and Gloria Gaither
- Dove Award, Gospel Songwriter of the Year, Bill Gaither
- Award, Honorary Citizen of Tennessee, Bill Gaither
- Dove Award, Inspirational Album of the Year, "Jesus, We Just Want to Thank You"

1977

- Dove Award, Gospel Songwriter of the Year, Bill Gaither
- General Assembly and Executive Council of the Church of God (Anderson, Indiana) Award for The Bill Gaither Trio's "invaluable contributions in composing, playing, singing, recording, and producing gospel music"
- "Alleluia! A Praise Gathering for Believers," album certified gold, RIAA

• Dove Award of Merit "in recognition of Bill Gaither's contribution to the world of gospel music"

1978
• Dove Award, Album of the Year (traditional), "Pilgrim's Progress"
• Dove Award, Album of the Year (inspirational), "Pilgrim's Progress"

1979
• Dove Award, Best Mixed Gospel Group of the Year, The Bill Gaither Trio
• Dove nomination for Song of the Year, "I Am Loved"
• Dove nomination, Album of the Year (Inspirational), "The Very Best of the Very Best, for Kids"
• Dove nomination, Gospel Songwriter of the Year, Bill Gaither

1980
• ASCAP Award of Merit, "I Am Loved"
• ASCAP nomination, Song of the Year, "I Am Loved"
• Dove Award, Best Mixed Group of the Year, The Bill Gaither Trio

1981
• Dove Award, Gospel Album of the Year, Children's Music, "The Very Best of the Very Best, for Kids"

1982
• Dove nomination for Gospel Album of the Year (Inspirational), The New Gaither Vocal Band

- Gospel Music Association Hall of Fame, Bill Gaither
- Children's Record Album of the Year, "Kids Under Construction"

1983
- Dove nomination, Best Inspirational Album, "The New Gaither Vocal Band"

1984
- Grammy nomination, Best Performance by a Duo or Group, "No Other Name But Jesus," The New Gaither Vocal Band
- Dove nomination, Best Inspirational Album, "Passin' the Faith Along," The Gaither Vocal Band

1985
- Dove Award, Gospel Music Album of the Year (Children's), "L-I-F-E," The Bill Gaither Trio and Ron Griffin
- Dove nomination, Gospel Music Album of the Year (Inspirational), "A New Point of View," The Gaither Vocal Band
- Dove nomination, Producer of the Year (Traditional), "Wherever I Am," The Talleys produced by Bill Gaither

1986
- Dove Award, Gospel Music Album of the Year (Worship and Praise), "I've Just Seen Jesus," Bill Gaither and Randy Vader
- Dove nomination, Gospel Music Album of the Year

(Inspirational), "Then He Said Sing," The Bill Gaither Trio
• Dove nomination, Gospel Music Album of the Year (Musical), "Then Came the Morning," produced by Bill Gaither and Randy Vader
• Dove nomination, Gospel Song of the Year, "I've Just Seen Jesus"
• Mayor's Chief Anderson Award for Enhancing Nationwide Community Recognition

1991

• Dove Award, Southern Gospel Recorded Song of the Year, "Climbing Higher and Higher," The Cathedrals produced by Bill Gaither, Mark Trammell, and Lari Goss

1992

• Grammy Award, Best Southern Gospel Album, "Homecoming," The Gaither Vocal Band
• National Association of Evangelicals, Laypersons of the Year Award, Bill and Gloria Gaither
• Dove Award, Best Southern Gospel Album, "Homecoming," The Gaither Vocal Band